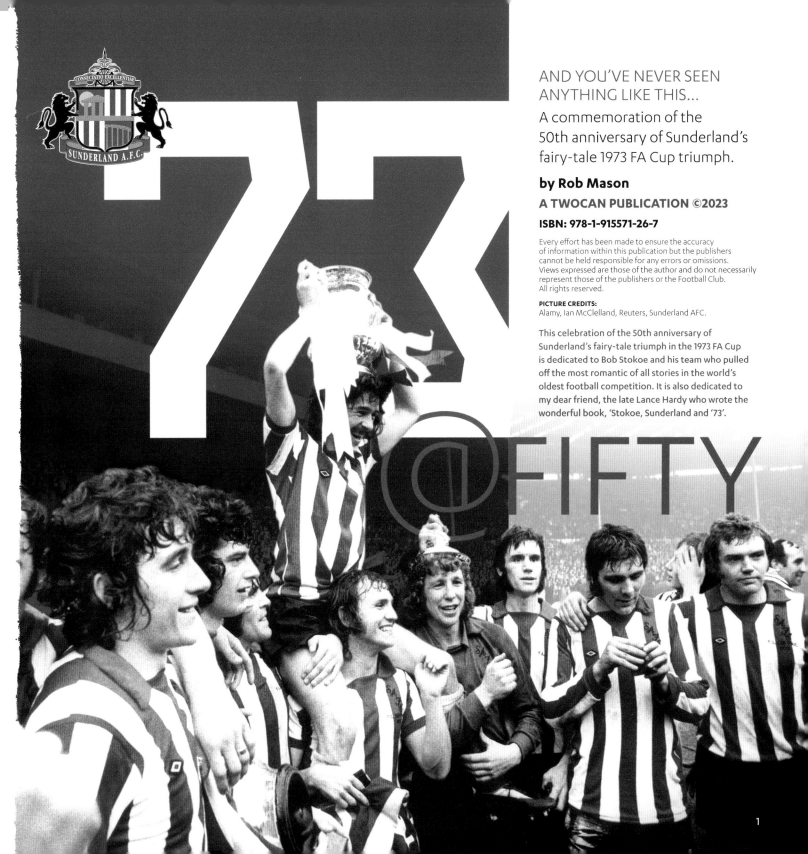

AND YOU'VE NEVER SEEN ANYTHING LIKE THIS...

A commemoration of the 50th anniversary of Sunderland's fairy-tale 1973 FA Cup triumph.

by Rob Mason

A TWOCAN PUBLICATION ©2023

ISBN: 978-1-915571-26-7

PICTURE CREDITS:
Alamy, Ian McClelland, Reuters, Sunderland AFC.

This celebration of the 50th anniversary of Sunderland's fairy-tale triumph in the 1973 FA Cup is dedicated to Bob Stokoe and his team who pulled off the most romantic of all stories in the world's oldest football competition. It is also dedicated to my dear friend, the late Lance Hardy who wrote the wonderful book, 'Stokoe, Sunderland and '73'.

FOREWORD: KAREN CRAVEN, Bob Stokoe's daughter

Sunderland's FA Cup win of 1973 was amazing. Considering the teams they beat, the way they beat them and how low Sunderland had been in the second division before the cup run started there has never been a cup story to match it.

I was 13 at the time and there was very much a family atmosphere at the Club. I got to know all the players and their wives and due to the fact that I spent my teenage years with them have always considered them to be my friends. In a way you could say that I "grew up" with the '73 team. I even went to school with one of Bobby Kerr's daughters, though she was quite a lot younger than me.

Football always came first for my dad. As a family we were never made to feel second but football came first. Even after he retired, when he scouted for Ian Porterfield when Ian was manager of Chelsea, dad loved his football. Part of the reason my parents moved house from Carlisle to Bury was because there were more teams to look at in the north-west and it was easier to get to a lot of games during the years he was scouting.

His love of football never went away and his affinity with Sunderland was very important to him. He had won the FA Cup as a player with Newcastle United where he started his career and he always said he was black and white down one half and red and white down the other! He loved Sunderland and loved managing in the north-east. He was so proud to bring the FA Cup to Wearside.

As a young girl I wasn't allowed to go to the final. My dad said there would be no other children there so my grandparents, my dad's parents, came to babysit. My grandma took the dog out for a two hour walk while the final was on as she could not bear the tension and I watched the match on the television with my grandad and we were ecstatic when we won!

Although I wasn't allowed to go to the final, I was on the team bus when the team brought the trophy back on the Tuesday after winning at Wembley. The players were all at the front but my mam and I were at the back all the way from Durham where the journey began. It was just incredible. It seemed as if everyone from the north-east was there.

Along with my husband Malc I travel up from Bury to most home matches. I have a big soft spot for Sunderland and always appreciated the invitation Sir Bob Murray gave to me come to the first game after my dad passed away, which appropriately enough was an FA Cup tie with Birmingham in 2004. I like to think that every time I'm at the match I bring the love of my dad with me.

73

@FIFTY

KAREN WITH JEAN STOKOE AND THE FAMILY DOG JED

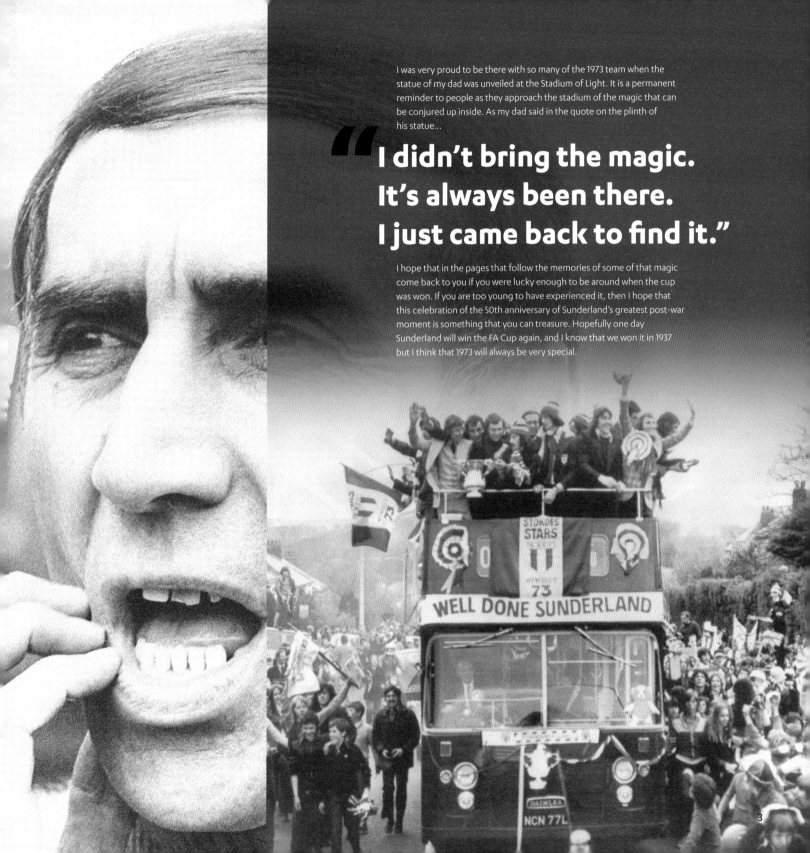

I was very proud to be there with so many of the 1973 team when the statue of my dad was unveiled at the Stadium of Light. It is a permanent reminder to people as they approach the stadium of the magic that can be conjured up inside. As my dad said in the quote on the plinth of his statue...

"I didn't bring the magic. It's always been there. I just came back to find it."

I hope that in the pages that follow the memories of some of that magic come back to you if you were lucky enough to be around when the cup was won. If you are too young to have experienced it, then I hope that this celebration of the 50th anniversary of Sunderland's greatest post-war moment is something that you can treasure. Hopefully one day Sunderland will win the FA Cup again, and I know that we won it in 1937 but I think that 1973 will always be very special.

The story of Sunderland's FA Cup win in 1973 is the stuff of legend.

A side that had struggled in the first half of the season after years in the doldrums was revitalised by the arrival of Bob Stokoe, the man who became known as the Messiah.

EVENING CHRONICLE
CUP FINAL PINK
No. 29,859 · SATURDAY, MAY 5, 1973

Sunderland fight like lions to topple the holders

WE'VE WON!

SUNDERLAND 1
LEEDS 0

SUNDERLAND, you were magnifi-
t. Superb. All heart and guts.
ould ask for no more
today.

LONDON EDITION
No. 31,601 (100th YEAR)

THEY'

This was the vital first goal which came after 31 minutes. Th

Porterfield hero in glo
Wembl

73 @FIFTY

Sunderland were transformed from a club very much down on its heels to the most celebrated team on the planet. In 1973 the FA Cup retained a worldwide magnetism and the story of Sunderland beating Leeds United at the culmination of an incredible cup-run captured the imagination of the global sporting public. In the five decades since then the players who made the impossible happen have rightly become regarded as true legends of the game and Sunderland in particular.

Hopefully this book will reinforce their place in the club's history. As always, the writing of a book requires help from many people. Firstly I wish to offer thanks to all of the players who so willingly shared their memories. This applies not only to the Sunderland players but also those from the clubs Sunderland defeated to win the trophy. Players from all six of the clubs Sunderland played have contributed to this book.

I would also like to thank Bob Stokoe's daughter Karen Craven for writing the Foreword and also for the loan of some of her family photographs. My thanks also go to supporters Joe Anderson, Malcolm Bramley, Derek Carter and Mike Love for their memories of 1973, as well as veteran journalist Doug Weatherall who was very close to the cup team at the time. My thanks also go to Andrew Smithson, Mike Gibson and Barry Jackson who have all worked with me on numerous books and whose support is invariably invaluable. I also thank twocan for their support of the project as both designers and publishers. I am indebted to Sir Bob Murray for his assistance in putting me in touch with Eddie Gray of Leeds United. Further thanks go to Ron Grant of the Former Players' Association of Reading FC, Nick Richardson of Notts County, Dr Michael Chappell, the Honorary Club Historian of Notts County and Mark Andrews of thearsenalhistory.com

Thanks to Ian McClelland who took the photographs at the Freedom of the City event in 2022 and to Steve Davison and Sharon Ewart of Sunderland AFC for their work in staging the 50th anniversary Gala Dinner at the Stadium of Light on 5 May 2023 that I proposed and organised in line with this publication.

Rob Mason
November 2022

Echo
—SUNDERLAND

SPORTS EDITION

SATURDAY, MAY 5, 1973   3p

E DONE IT!

who scored was Ian Porterfield

CUP FINAL SPECIAL

the ious

MEANWHILE
BACK IN
SUNDERLAND

HARTLEPOOL V
SCUNTHORPE U.

MONDAY, NOVEMBER 27th, 1972

5p

ROKER PARK GROUND

ALAN BROWN

BILLY ELLIOTT

BILLY ELLIOTT

73 @FIFTY

November 1972 wasn't all that dissimilar to November 2022. In 1972 November had seen rampant inflation result in the government of Conservative Prime Minister Ted Heath introduce a freeze on wages as well as prices and rents. On the 28th November the Cabinet met the leaders of the National Union of Mineworkers who had been taking industrial action since the 12th of the month. The miners represented included those employed at Wearmouth Colliery on the site of what is now The Stadium of Light. Times were hard but some of those miners would have been at Roker Park the night before the NUM met the government to watch FA Cup action.

Sunderland weren't playing. The game was a second round second replay between Len Ashurst's Hartlepool United and a Scunthorpe United side which included Neil Warnock. Hartlepool lost 2-1 in extra-time in front of a crowd of just over 7,000. The previous match at Roker Park had seen a fraction over 11,000 die-hards witness a second division draw between Sunderland and Hull City. The Wearsiders were without a manager, fifties stalwart Billy Elliott was standing in as caretaker following the sacking of Alan Brown. After a miserable defeat at Bristol City, as the end of the month approached Sunderland were 19th in the table, only outside the relegation zone on goal average.

It wasn't a great time. Life was hard. There wasn't much money about on Wearside. A good chunk of the town's main thoroughfare, Fawcett Street, was boarded up after demolition work to the former Town Hall. Unemployment was high and the football club, so often the oasis of escapism for people in tough times, was only making things worse. Relegated in 1970, there seemed little hope of a return to the top-flight anytime soon.

Even in poor seasons football-wise, the turn of the calendar year offered renewed hope in the shape of the FA Cup. In 1972 Sunderland had been drawn at home to Leeds United in the fifth round. The problem was they still had to beat Cardiff City in round four, the Welsh side eventually progressing to face Leeds after knocking Sunderland out in a second replay at Manchester City's Maine Road on a Wednesday afternoon. Such was the allure of the Cup that at a time when league crowds had seen only just over 8,000 at the most recent home game, over 39,000 piled into Roker Park for the first replay with Cardiff. This was despite the game being played on a Monday afternoon, floodlights being banned due to a miners' strike biting at the energy supply. That tie with Cardiff ended 1-1 with Sunderland going down 3-1 48 hours later in Manchester on an afternoon when barely a thousand more than would see Hartlepool play Scunthorpe at Roker turned up.

Sunderland did not get to face Leeds in 1972. That clash would take place on the grandest of stages at the end of the following season. A decade earlier there had been no special rivalry with Leeds. All that changed in 1962-63. Under Don Revie Leeds were in the early stages of becoming the most reviled side in the country. They were in the process of developing into a fabulously talented football team but one haunted by any admiration for their ability being tainted by their style of play. This was thought by many to be downright dirty and combined with the beginnings of gamesmanship that now is sadly commonplace, but then was thankfully rare.

As Leeds left the field at Elland Road after beating Sunderland 1-0 very early in the '62-63 season they emerged as victors against ten men. In those days before substitutes young Sunderland forward Willie McPheat had been stretchered off with a broken leg after what was described as a horror challenge by Leeds' Bobby Collins.

The relationship between the clubs didn't get any better. The following season in 1963-64 they were promoted together, Leeds pipping Sunderland for the Division Two title but Sunderland earning a win and a draw against Don Revie's team.

Once promoted, Leeds soared as Sunderland struggled. The clubs clashed in the FA Cup in the fifth round in 1966-67. This time Bobby Kerr suffered a broken leg. It came in a collision with Norman 'Bites Yer Legs' Hunter, although this time it was by all accounts an accident. An aggregate attendance of over 154,000 saw this tie including what is still Leeds' record attendance of 57,892 for the first replay. In the second replay at Hull City's Boothferry Park all hell broke loose when with the score level with three minutes remaining referee Ken Stokes gave Leeds a highly questionable penalty which was converted by Johnny Giles.

In a bitterly contested game there was still time for Stokes to send off Sunderland men George Herd and George Mulhall. The official had to be given a police escort off the pitch with Mulhall adamant until his death that the game was not 'straight'. Come the 1973 FA Cup final six of the 12 named by Leeds at Hull were in their Wembley side with only Montgomery of Sunderland surviving, though injury victim Kerr had also played in the tie.

"They were just so cynical. It was win at all costs and it didn't matter who they trod on" says Bournemouth based Sunderland supporter Joe Anderson who was then living in Essex. "The 1970 FA Cup final against Chelsea showed just how much of a dirty side they were. Players like Norman Hunter and Billy Bremner were great players but they were just disliked all over the country. West Ham and Orient were my local teams at the time and their supporters were like everyone else in that they despised Leeds. People didn't like their fans either. They weren't shrinking violets!"

As Bob Stokoe arrived as Sunderland manager on 29 November 1972 Sunderland and Leeds were more miles apart in footballing terms than the 96 miles that separate the places. While Sunderland had slumped to that defeat at Bristol City's Ashton Gate on the previous weekend Leeds had been waltzing to a 3-0 home win over Manchester City. This extended their unbeaten top-flight run to eight games. They had also progressed to round four of the League Cup and round three of the European Cup Winners' Cup.

As Stokoe took over the reins at Roker it seemed incomprehensible that the following season it would be Sunderland who would be competing in the European Cup Winners' Cup! So far in the season their solitary cup appearance had seen them well beaten by holders Stoke in the League Cup.

Things can change quickly in football. Rarely, if ever, have they changed so dramatically and successfully as they did following Stokoe's arrival.

73

@FIFTY

WILLIE McPHEAT

Famously Stokoe's first decision was to change the colour of the shorts. Sunderland had traditionally worn black shorts. Alan Brown had changed these to white in his first spell in charge and George Hardwick and Ian McColl had continued with that choice during their mid-sixties spells as manager. Brown had continued with white shorts during his second stint in charge but remembering Sunderland had always worn black shorts in his playing days Stokoe immediately ordered a return to black. No-one knew this until the team ran out of the tunnel for the new manager's first match but it immediately curried favour with the fans.

The shorts weren't the only thing to change colour during Stokoe's first season. At the time every sizeable town or city had its own Saturday sports paper. This would be rapidly printed and distributed the moment the final scores were announced. Victims of the digital era and instant news, 'Football Echo's' are sadly no more. For generations of fans they were essential reading every weekend. Traditionally printed on pink paper, Sunderland's Sports Echo had changed to a pale blue in shock when Sunderland were relegated and had later went white. It proudly returned to pink on the night of the cup final. As well as going on sale in the north east, special additions of the paper bearing a logo of an aeroplane were flown to London and sold to joyous Wearsiders, and no doubt to intrigued Londoners too.

Capital copies of the 'Football' Echo were a long way off as Burnley beat Sunderland in Stokoe's first match. The Turf Moor club were en-route to winning the division and were too good for Sunderland on the day. A week later the contingent of Sunderland supporters in a feeble crowd of 5,783 at Portsmouth needed to see a new manager bounce in what was a relegation battle. Third bottom Pompey were level on points with Sunderland going into the game where the prospect of defeat offered calamitous consequences. With four minutes to go at Fratton Park it was looking like a depressingly lengthy journey home as Sunderland trailed 2-1. The turnaround was to be a microcosm of what would happen in the season as goals from Billy Hughes and Bobby Kerr in the closing minutes transformed disaster into delight.

Following a goalless home draw with Preston North End Stokoe had a stroke of luck. It may not have seemed like it as several members of his squad went down with flu. It meant the postponement of three fixtures. It allowed Stokoe time to reflect on and assess his new squad after seeing them in three games. It also gave him the chance to work with those players not struck down by illness.

When play resumed on the first Saturday of 1973 Sunderland were revitalised, beating Brighton 4-0 for the biggest win of the season. Seven days later the cup campaign began with a hard fought draw at Notts County with the Division Three outfit attracting over 30,000 to the replay - well over twice the size of the previous gate.

A replay was also needed in the fourth round where the main focus of interest was on the return to Roker of Reading manager Charlie Hurley. When Sunderland were drawn away to Manchester City or Liverpool there was excitement at a glamorous cup tie against one of the country's leading sides.

The beauty of the FA Cup is that no matter how big a team you are you can be beaten by a minnow. Only the previous season top-flight Newcastle United had been humiliated in a replay defeat at non-league Hereford United. While there was always a glimmer of hope as huge numbers of the red and white army headed for Maine Road; where cup hopes had ended against Cardiff the previous year, those who were red and white realists realised that in all likelihood the afternoon would be one of damage limitation. Had Sunderland put up a gallant fight and lost without being hammered many would have thought it was the conclusion of a decent cup run and would have enjoyed an afternoon back at a big-time club.

Heads may have said City but hearts said Sunderland and Sunderland played with such heart that they fully merited the draw they earned. Bringing City back to Roker Park under the lights encouraged hopes that an upset might be achieved, especially in the light of the Lads performance in Manchester.

Nothing could have prepared City for what awaited them. The Roker Roar was at its most fearsome as City were swept away despite their attempted fightback when two down.

As fans made their way home, after witnessing a game voted the ground's 'Match of the Century' almost quarter of a century later, news of Sunderland's performance spread like wildfire. Without mobile phones or the internet it was largely word of mouth that told of how sensationally Sunderland had played. Cup fever was now rapidly spreading across Wearside.

Before the replay kicked-off people knew that the prize was a quarter-final at home to Luton Town, the only other second division team left in the competition. Get past City and there was a definite chance of Sunderland reaching the semi-finals for the first time since before the club's first-ever relegation in the fifties. Once the Lads eased past Luton Town and had the prospect of Arsenal at Hillsborough cup fever rose more and more.

Six seasons earlier a bit of Sunderland had had a recent foretaste of cup fever. Wearside League Ryhope Colliery Welfare had won through to the first round proper of the FA Cup and had pulled the plum tie of Football League outfit Workington at home. Ryhope went cup crazy. Shops were bedecked in the red and white of Ryhope with the grand Co-op stores covered in huge red and white drapes. Local butchers provided free steaks to the players (how pre-match meals have changed) and all anyone wanted to talk about was the Workington cup-tie (which resulted in a 1-0 defeat on a frozen pitch).

Now the whole of Sunderland and the heartlands of the Durham coalfield had cup fever. Sunderland was still part of County Durham at this point and in footballing terms is still traditionally and proudly County Durham's club. Shops and the windows of peoples' houses started to become bedecked in red and white regalia. In the case of my house in Ryhope you couldn't see out of the front room window for weeks. It was plastered with pictures of Stokoe and his stars, combined with red and white scarves, ribbons and rosettes.

RYHOPE C.W. SUPPORTERS' CLUB
GRAND FOOTBALL MATCH
F.A. Challenge Cup.
1st. Round Proper
RYHOPE C.W.
v
WORKINGTON TOWN
on RYHOPE C.W. GROUND
SATURDAY DECEMBER 9th. 1967
Kick Off · 2-15 p.m.
ADMISSION TO GROUND 4/-
(Admission by Ticket Only)

Referee: K. STYLES, Barnsley.
Linesmen:
SGT. R. P. COLEMAN, Ripon.   K. R. HORNCASTLE, York.
President: E. MAGGIORE.
Vice-Presidents:
Dr. R. H. HENDERSON and J. REED.
Chairman: J. L. LOWE.
Secretary: J. ERRINGTON.
Treasurer: L. L. Etherington.
Committee:
J. Wilkinson, Snr., J. Graham, T. Nicholson, U. Nicholson, W. Nicholson,
D. Miller, P. Bogan (Trainer), J. Carlin, T. Chambers, J. Golden, T. Rathburn.

PROGRAMME
No. 1827

PRICE 6d.

This wasn't my doing, it was my mam's. Like everyone else she was as proud as punch and once Arsenal became the latest victims of the cup run and Sunderland had the cup final to look forward to the town (Sunderland was still a town until the year of their next FA Cup final appearance in 1992) became frenzied.

Whereas a few months earlier you would have struggled to get some people to go to the match if you'd made admission free, now everyone wanted to go. Those who had loyally supported Sunderland during the thin times became anxious that they would miss out on a cup final ticket to the thousands upon thousands of previously missing supporters who had returned now that Sunderland had a team worth supporting.

A voucher system had been introduced at league games. These were lettered vouchers with a lucky draw then revealing which vouchers were valid to qualify the holders for a cup ticket. The voucher system was a clever marketing idea for the club as it gave supporters an extra reason to attend league matches but it did little to protect the interests of those supporters who had continued to turn up regularly during the bad times. Other than season ticket holders who were guaranteed a cup final ticket there was probably no fair way of doing this, but for those fans who had never missed a game for years and now faced missing the biggest game of them all it led to desperation and at times despair.

Despite money being incredibly tight for most people, black market tickets were in high demand. Sunderland supporters didn't take too kindly to being fleeced by London touts however, the Sports Echo reporting on cup final day that one group of Sunderland supporters had chased some ticket touts on the approaches to Olympic Way leading to the stadium and grabbed a number of tickets.

The cup run had a dramatic effect on life on Wearside. Despite the bleak economic outlook the success of the football team had finally put the sun into Sunderland. People had smiles on their faces, people were happy and people were proud.

Economic output mushroomed. There was no better example of this than at the colliery where the Stadium of Light now stands. 2,200 men were employed at Wearmouth pit at the time. Late in 1972, before the cup-run got going between 30 and 35 hundredweights of coal was being produced per manshift. By the time of the cup final that had increased to between 40 and 44 hundredweight!

It was a similar story in the shipyards. At Austin & Pickersgill productivity was dramatically increased, leading to chairman and managing director Derek B Kimber commenting, "I think morale goes up when the local football team is doing well." A spokesman at Thorn Radio Tube and Valves Limited in Sunderland agreed, "There does seem to be a more congenial atmosphere and better spirit on the shop floor since the football team started doing so well." My own dad was a shop steward and branch secretary in the Amalgamated Union of Engineering Workers at Doxfords shipyards. His District Secretary Harry Wilkinson summed it up, "There is no doubt about it.

All industrial problems are resolved when the football team is doing well. People just don't realise how seriously working men take their football."

Wearside women take their football seriously as well of course but Wilkinson continued, "If the team have lost ...they just don't feel like working. They feel bitterness and sourness towards the club's directors. They curse about the players. But what a different story it is when the team win. The Hallelujahs produce a greater willingness to work than the post-mortems. If the team wins the cup and looks forward to promotion next year the employers of Sunderland will be queueing up to make donations to Roker Park because of the greater effort they are going to get from their men."

Thankfully some Sunderland statistics went down during the cup run. The Samaritans reported a considerable decrease in calls in Sunderland from March to May 1973 while the local Citizens Advice Bureau also recorded a marked reduction in cases, especially regarding personal and family problems.

Tyne Tees Television produced an iconic documentary on cup final day. Entitled, 'Meanwhile Back in Sunderland' it focussed on those ticketless fans left back in Sunderland who watched the cup final on TV or on huge screens. It began with shots of excited supporters leaving early in the morning by bus or train. One of the people interviewed at the railway station - although unnamed in the programme - was John Tennick. John was a legendary supporter who for many years organised the Supporters' Association coaches to away games which left from his fishing tackle shop in Dundas Street a few goal-kicks away from Roker Park.

On the day Sunderland had been knocked out of the cup in 1972 I travelled with John by train to Manchester for that second replay with Cardiff. It was so long ago that we were in one of those old fashioned carriages with compartments that sat about six people. John had seen it all. He was Sunderland through and through, as good and as knowledgeable supporter as you could ever wish to meet.

In 'Meanwhile Back in Sunderland' he says, "It's absolutely fabulous. Right on top of the world. Everybody's walking on air. Everybody wants to be in on the red and whites. It's absolutely wonderful, the support that they're giving down here. I've never known anything like it in this town in all of my 60 years. It's been absolutely beyond anything you could imagine."

As he so often was, John Tennick was right. If you are old enough to have been there you will have never forgotten the atmosphere on Wearside at that time, not just on matchdays. If you were born in the years that followed and have read and heard about the magic of Stokoe's Stars then everything you have heard is true - and then some. It was the most amazing and incredible time. If you go to the match in 2023 and hear the crowd singing, "Wise Men Say, Only Fools Rush In, But I Can't Help Falling In Love With You," 1973 was the time when people fell back in love with SAFC. In the half century since it is these memories of 1973 that have done so much to sustain the love and support of Sunderland through the good times and the bad.

73 @FIFTY

THE STADIUM OF LIGHT NOW STANDS
ON THE SITE OF WEARMOUTH COLLIERY
WHICH DRAMATICALLY INCREASED ITS
PRODUCTION DURING THE 1973 FA CUP RUN

If you have never seen 'Meanwhile Back In Sunderland', or even if you have, I recommend that you go and make yourself a drink, google the 25 minute programme and watch it before reading the rest of '73@fifty'. It is a marvellous programme that totally captures what football is to Sunderland. Don't forget to have a handkerchief ready because it will bring tears, but they will be tears of joy.

MALCOLM BRAMLEY

Former assistant secretary at Sunderland who at the time had been club secretary to Brian Clough at Derby and was about to take on the same role for Len Ashurst at Gillingham.

"It was a surprise to everybody really because there was no indication before the cup run that we remotely had any chance. Gradually we came to realise we had a group of players who were totally committed to each other. You could see the 100% that everyone was giving in every game. It was so long since we'd had a bit of hope that something might be happening at Sunderland. At the final as well as our own fans there was so much backing from all of the neutral fans because we were playing Leeds and Leeds weren't liked."

DEREK CARTER

Sunderland supporter.

"At the start of 1973 I was in no doubt whatsoever that it was destined to be a memorable year, although my confident prediction was based solely on the fact that I'd signed up for the Royal Navy rather than any dreams of football success. After all, we were a club struggling at the bottom end of the second tier so for anyone to even suggest we'd win the FA Cup beating Man City, Arsenal and Leeds would have resulted in hysterical laughter. However, against all the odds we did it and when Bobby Kerr picked up that famous trophy it was a moment when total disbelief resounded throughout the footballing world but back in Sunderland, tears were shed, random strangers were hugged and it was party time.

The season started off very poorly but when Bob Stokoe arrived at the end of November it proved to be the biggest and longest 'new manager bounce' in the history of the club. The Lads had a new lease of life and started producing the goods although it still took a little while before the crowds began to believe. That moment came when we were drawn against the mighty Manchester City in the fifth round of the FA Cup."

"We'd had a couple of scares in the previous rounds, especially against Reading who were managed by Sunderland legend Charlie Hurley. Their goalkeeper had the game of his life that day, which was somewhat ironic as his surname was Death and even though we won through, we were massive underdogs as we headed to Maine Road to face the stars such as Summerbee, Bell, Marsh and Lee. We took the game to them from the off which earned us a deserved draw and the replay was one of the greatest games I've ever witnessed.

73@FIFTY

The atmosphere was fantastic and some of the comments from the City manager and players suggesting they just had to turn up to win certainly added spice to the occasion. We were magnificent and they were sent packing in front of over fifty thousand fans who had our old stadium rocking. We began to dream and after winning through against a stubborn Luton Town in the next round we headed off to Hillsborough to face Arsenal. They went the same way as City and we went from dreaming to believing.

"The final against Leeds turned out to be the greatest upset the FA Cup had ever seen. They were the team fans loved to hate, masters of the dark arts and a squad crammed full of fantastic players. There was no way we could win and according to the experts Eddie Gray was going to murder us on his own. Well what did they know? Ritchie Pitt took out star striker Alan 'Sniffer' Clarke with a lovely tackle in the first minute which led to him being totally anonymous, Dick Malone and Bobby Kerr marked Eddie Gray so well he was substituted and the Lads produced a sensational display of teamwork in front of a worldwide audience and outside of Leeds football lovers and purists rejoiced."

MIKE LOVE

Sunderland supporter.

"Having been successful in the ballot for tickets for both the quarter and semi-finals, I wasn't successful in obtaining a Final ticket. A pal at work told me that he knew a long distance lorry driver who drank in his local club had a ticket for the Leeds end that he was willing to sell. I ended up paying £8 for a £1 standing ticket and whilst I thought I could manage to keep my feelings in check the plan was to try and exchange for the Sunderland end once we arrived at Wembley.

What transpired was a scene reminiscent of a prisoner exchange at Checkpoint Charlie as I negotiated a swap with two Leeds skinheads. I don't think either party was totally convinced that this would work but after what seemed an eternity of showing and verifying the authenticity of the tickets, we finally exchanged much to my relief. We even exchanged best of luck messages which was very civil!

At least I was in the Sunderland end which was a huge bonus. This view took an odd turn as having entered into the standing pen I was kicked up the backside and pushed down three steps. Assuming things were kicking off I turned only to find three Sunderland pals from the Blyth/Cramlington area who thought that this would be a fitting way to introduce themselves!

Whilst standing in the queue waiting for the turnstiles to open a chorus of boos arose from those behind. Turning around we saw Jack Charlton, who was part of the Big Match panel making his way into the ground. A big cheer then went up as he was followed by Derek Dougan, who was sporting a Sunderland rosette. Dougan then proceeded to give Charlton the v-sign behind his back which drew and even larger cheer!"

"Charlton turned to see what the commotion was about only to be met by Dougan protesting his innocence and shrugging as if he didn't know what was going on! Pure comedy gold.

"We travelled down to Wembley on a Hunters coach from Seaton Delaval which left at midnight on the Friday night. The coach was festooned with Sunderland colours and bunting. Toilet facilities were provided by a single bucket situated at the front of the coach! Life's little luxuries!

I recall a guy from our village, who travelled to Wembley with us, used to put a bet on both Sunderland and Newcastle each year to win the FA Cup. He got 250/1 on Sunderland and then placed a second bet when the price came down to 175/1. I don't know how much he actually won but he treated everyone on the coach to a drink when we stopped off at a social club in Watford for a few celebratory drinks!

"The dislike between Leeds and Sunderland had probably started in the early sixties and was mainly about Leeds' win at all costs mentality. The 1967 FA Cup tie which resulted in Bobby Kerr fracturing his leg and the controversial winning goal from Leeds in the second replay helped fuel the animosity. During that period a number of opposition players had career threatening injuries when playing against Leeds including our own Willie McPheat and Newcastle's George Dalton and it was this mentality that brought about the 'Dirty Leeds' title that followed them around for many years.

Needless to say Leeds were disliked by most teams but they appeared to revel in the notoriety. It was because of this dislike that most fans gloated on the number of Leeds near misses when missing out on some of the major honours during the 1970s."

"The 1973 team will always be remembered for producing one of the greatest FA Cup adventures in history and are widely regarded both nationally and locally for one of the most amazing Cup wins of all time."

THE OTHER MAGPIES

ROUND 3

DATE: Saturday 13 January 1973

NOTTS COUNTY 1
Bradd 29

SUNDERLAND 1
Watson 79

ATTENDANCE: 15,142

73@FIFTY

DAVE WATSON HEADS SUNDERLAND'S EQUALISER AT NOTTS COUNTY.

Bob Stokoe had been in charge for four games before this tie got the cup-run under way. The man who came to be known as 'The Messiah' had taken over on 29 November. Four days later he had seen his new side go down 0-1 at home to a Burnley team en-route to becoming Second Division champions.

Mick Docherty, Colin Waldron, Doug Collins and Leighton James of the Burnley team that day would later play for Sunderland who would also make a strenuous but unsuccessful attempt to sign midfielder Alan West. The Clarets manager Jimmy Adamson would succeed Stokoe at Sunderland just under four years later (after Ian MacFarlane had bridged the gap as caretaker).

If the Burnley team that inflicted defeat on Stokoe on his first game was a glimpse into the future of SAFC the immediate future was about to be transformed. Eight of the players who faced the Clarets would be cup winners before Burnley played in the first division. Stokoe had already gone back to the future. His first decision as manager drew approval before the Burnley game even kicked off. As the teams ran out Sunderland were wearing the club's traditional black shorts. Since 1961 when manager Alan Brown introduced white shorts there had been no black in the Black Cats kit but instantly Stokoe had shown an understanding of the club's traditions. The club of course were not officially nicknamed the Black Cats until after the move to the Stadium of Light in 1997 but they had been associated with black cats since the early days of the club and indeed a black cat has been the emblem of the Supporters' Association since it started in 1965.

Losing 0-1 to top of the table Burnley was not judged a disaster although defeat left Sunderland fourth bottom. The crowd of 16,812 was pretty much 50% more than the 11,141 who had witnessed the previous home match. The attraction of seeing the promotion pacesetters had helped with the increased gate but mostly the additions were those delighted to have a new manager. Within three months that new manager would have crowds of over 50,000 squeezing into Roker Park after not so much waking the sleeping giant as giving it an electric shock to jolt it into life.

New manager bounces need a good start. Losing narrowly to the league leaders straight after taking over was one thing but defeat a week later at Portsmouth, who had not won at home since September, would have meant Sunderland's lowly league position would get even worse and the potential impact of a new leader had been lost. The prospect of a fight against a first-ever relegation to the third tier would be the likelihood for 1973 rather than the greatest few months in the club's post-war history. Half a century on it is still the greatest few months since the war.

Fewer than six thousand were at Fratton Park, the scene of Sunderland's first-ever relegation in 1958. Most of those were happy as Pompey led 2-1 with four minutes left as the diehards who had travelled on the Supporters' Association's buses organised by John Tennick prepared for the 330 mile return journey. That trip was made a joyous one when Billy Hughes and Bobby Kerr scored in the 87th and 89th minutes to add to Dave Watson's first-half opener.

After five away losses in a row Sunderland had won on the road. Suddenly that 330 mile trip home was welcomed as there was a victory to savour from the town where HMS Victory resides. Christmas was coming and unknown to the world the man in red and white was about to deliver untold delight.

That delight had to wait a little while. Seven days later Sunderland kept home fans waiting for the first home goal of the Stokoe era as a goalless draw was played against Bobby Charlton's Preston North End. It was then that a flu-bug struck Sunderland. The best timed flu-bug possible. Sunderland would not play again until 6 January. Three games were called off but it gave Stokoe time to plan and work with the players who were not bed-ridden. When the Lads next took to the field Brighton were on the receiving end of the biggest win of the season as a 4-0 win provided a foretaste of what was to come.

A big following of supporters travelled to Meadow Lane for the opening game in the cup run away to third division Notts County. They had progressed beyond non-league Altrincham and Lancaster to reach the third round but had been struggling in the league. At Christmas they had been 17th but since then had won two home games and drawn away as they ran into form. That form would continue with a run to rival Sunderland's as they went on to storm to promotion. They had also shown cup pedigree by reaching the League Cup quarter-finals before Christmas having knocked out two top-flight sides in Southampton and Stoke. Managed by club legend Jimmy Sirrel, Notts were no pushovers.

THE GAME

Reporting on the match 'Argus' of the Football Echo would be on the telephone to a copytaker back at the Echo HQ, giving a kick by kick account of the game for that evening's sports paper. The moment his final words were taken down and the rest of the results were obtained the paper would be rushed onto the printing presses and copies bundled into vans. These would screech around the area getting the newspaper into shops sometimes as soon as within an hour of the final whistle. Remarkable work in the pre-internet/mobile phone age. There was no time for a rewrite of the front page which included the first part of the match report with the final section of the account of the game on the back page. Although the headline was updated to announce, 'Watson goal keeps Roker men in Cup' evidently Argus thought the Lads were going out when he penned his introductory lines, "Sunderland were on the losing end of a physical battle against Notts County in their third round FA Cup-tie at Meadow Lane this afternoon. They were lucky to be only one goal down after a first-half pounding which saw Bradd (29 minutes) grab only one of several clear-cut chances shaped against a hesitant Sunderland".

The Nottingham Football Post agreed. Its second paragraph read, "There was no denying that the Magpies were the superior side in the first half and Sunderland were fortunate to be only one goal in arrears at the halfway stage."

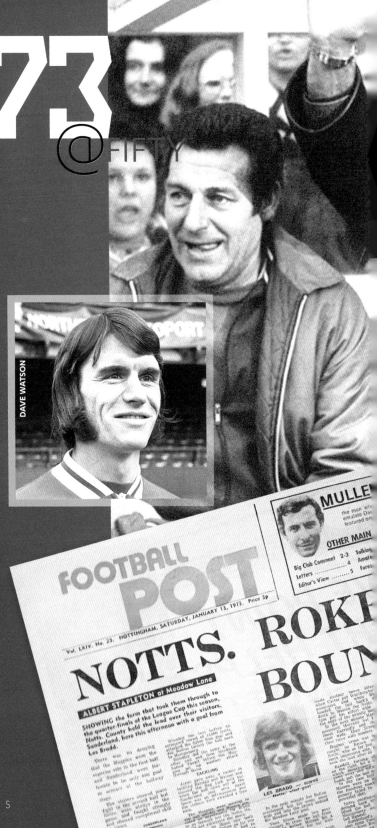

DAVE WATSON

TRAINER BILLY ELLIOTT, MANAGER BOB STOKOE, COACH ARTHUR COX AND PHYSIO JOHNNY WATTERS

Echo SUNDERLAND

No. 11,566 (100th YEAR)

SPORTS EDITION

SATURDAY, JANUARY 13, 1973   3p

Watson goal keeps Roker men in Cup

JOHN LATHAN

RICHIE PITT

FIVE FOR SALE

KEITH COLEMAN

Notts County - - - 1   Sunderland - - - - 1

SUNDERLAND were on the losing end of a physical battle against Notts County in their third round F.A. Cup-tie at Meadow Lane this afternoon. They were lucky to be only one goal down after a first half pounding which saw Bradd (29 minutes) grab only one of the several clear-cut chances shaped against a hesitant Sunderland.

Odd flashes from Hughes and Tueart proved that a resolute County defence could be cracked, but Sunderland were too busily engaged in defensive conflict to throw a great deal of support forward, though they were obviously determined to correct this in their spirited opening to the second half.

MANAGER Bob Stokoe today announced that Sunderland have decided on a mid-season pruning of their staff and named five young players, all with first team experience, who are now available for transfer.

They are: Derek Forster, Richie Pitt, Brian Chambers, Keith Coleman, and John Lathan.

All are youth team products and three of them — Forster, Pitt and Lathan — have played First Division football.

Mr Stokoe said: "We are circularizing clubs advising them that we will consider offers. We are not naming any figure and if after a time there have been no reasonable offers we will consider letting them go on loan to any club which needs help.

"These are all young players with first team experience and in the present situation things have come to a bit of a standstill for them. This is ...

BY ARGUS

NOTTS - 0
1 Brown
2 Bromley
3 Worthington
4 Masson
5 Needham
6 Stubbs
7 Nixon
8 Randall
9 Bradd
10 Mann
11 Carter
Sub: Bolton (1)

SUNDERLAND
Montgomery
Malone
Bolton (J)
Horswill
Watson
Pitt
Kerr
Ashurst
Hughes
Porterfield
Tueart
Sub: McIlvroe

Referee: Mr J Rice of Preston

Tueart came in at No. 8 for David Young, who is not eligible for this round of the Cup under the 14-day signing rule, and manager Bob Stokoe brought in Jackie Ashurst as an additional mid-field ...

Sunderland ... made ... three ... changes from ...

21

Although Sunderland improved in the second half, what became the most glorious of cup runs - not just for Sunderland but in the entire history of the FA Cup - almost ended at the first hurdle. Had Sunderland lost at Notts there would be no Stokoe statue at the Stadium of Light, Gordon Banks' 1970 save for defending champions England against Pele at the World Cup would be the greatest save in the history of English football, instead of the second greatest, and the fairytale of 1973 would never have materialised. The sleeping giant would have simply turned over and slept some more.

Monty's magical double-save at Wembley we will discuss fully later. It was a fantastic save on the biggest stage. Supporters who had not come back when the good times returned but had been there all the time knew that when the Mighty Jim pulled off the cup-final save that made him a household name it was not necessarily the greatest in Monty's marvellous catalogue of stunning saves. It was simply destined to become the most famous because it was in the final. Unlike that day at Wembley the third round tie at third division Notts County was not beamed around the world but on 5 May 1973 the world would have been watching Leeds United play someone else if it was not for Monty.

Shortly before Dave Watson headed the late equaliser that ruined Argus' intro Montgomery had kept Sunderland in the tie. The Nottingham Post recorded, "Montgomery certainly saved Sunderland when he made a fantastic save from a close range header from Bradd after Masson had made the opening". The Echo's correspondent incorrectly thought it was Kevin Randall Monty made that save from but he did a good job of describing Jim's handiwork, "It was a near thing when Masson centred from the right and Randall got to a header which whipped past Montgomery and looked a certain goal until the goalkeeper, diving back to the far post, managed to palm the ball out".

Trust me, if you are too young to have seen Monty he was simply the most spectacular and fantastic goalkeeper. He's always been my favourite player and he always will be. 'The Mighty Jim' indeed. Monty's magic provided the platform for Sunderland to level and take the first step on what proved to be the most joyful of journeys.

There were eleven minutes left when Dave Watson scored with a towering header against his first club to set up a replay in which Sunderland would progress without the problems posed at Meadow Lane. Sunderland played nine games to win the cup beating three of the best sides in the country but at no time after this first match did the Lads look like losing.

NOTTS COUNTY: Brown, Brindley, Worthington, Masson, Needham, Stubbs, Nixon, Bradd, Randall, Mann, Carter. Unused sub: Bolton.

SUNDERLAND: Montgomery, Malone, Bolton, Tones, Watson, Ashurst (McGiven), Horswill, Kerr, Hughes, Porterfield, Tueart.

REFEREE: Mr Jack Rice (Lancs).

*David Young - who would be twelfth man at Wembley - was not eligible to play as he had been signed (from Newcastle United) within 14 days of this game.

73@FIFTY

ROUND 3 REPLAY

DATE: Tuesday 16 January 1973

SUNDERLAND 2
Watson 54, Tueart 90

NOTTS COUNTY 0

ATTENDANCE: 30,033

There was only one change to the Meadow Lane starting line-ups. Mick McGiven came in for Jackie Ashurst with John Lathan replacing McGiven on the bench. Notts were unchanged. What did change was the nature of the match. On home turf Sunderland had by far the better of the exchanges although a confident Notts did pose the occasional problem.

For all their superiority Sunderland did not go ahead until nine minutes after half-time when Dave Watson was once again the scourge of his old club, this time scoring with a right-foot shot after being found by Ian Porterfield.

The second goal did not arrive until the last minute when live-wire Dennis Tueart robbed centre-back David Needham - a future England 'B' cap - to make the scoreline a better reflection of the night's work.

An attendance of over 30,000 produced gate receipts of £13,280, an indication that for all the inflation of half a century since then, football was a much more affordable sport to watch back in the days long before the Premier League.

SUNDERLAND: Montgomery, Malone, Bolton, Horswill (Lathan 87), Watson, Tones, Kerr, McGiven. Hughes, Porterfield, Tueart.

NOTTS COUNTY: Brown, Brindley, Worthington, Masson, Needham, Stubbs, Nixon, Bradd, Randall, Mann, Carter. Unused sub: Bolton.

REFEREE: Mr. Jack Rice (Lancs).

LES BRADD

Scored the first goal of the cup run -against Sunderland.

Notts goalscorer Les Bradd is Notts County's all-time leading scorer. As was normal in the seventies he took no prisoners. Bradd had been booked for a foul on Monty before Jim's great save and confirms Monty's great save was from him not Kevin Randall. Les says, "My recollections of that tie are first to do with the crowds, about 15,000 at Notts and twice that at Roker Park. I've got more recollections of the replay at Roker Park. There are two grounds where I played and had a bit of a headache from the noise. That is Roker Park and Villa Park. The noise came down and onto the pitch instead of up into the air. When things got going at Roker Park you certainly heard the noise down on the pitch. In the replay Sunderland were by far the better side and deserved to win easily. There wasn't much in the first match but there was no question they were the better side in the replay and obviously went on to win the cup which was fantastic for football.

" **I can remember scoring in the first half of the original tie past Jim Montgomery to put us in front. That kept us in the lead until late in the second half when Dave Watson was pushed up front and scored the equaliser."**

In particular Bradd remembers playing against Watson, "I remember Dave being pushed up as Sunderland chased an equaliser in the first match. I can still remember the manager shouting at him to go up and he went up and scored a goal. My first encounter with Dave was when I played against him in August 1967. He was centre-half and I was centre-forward when I scored in a 1-0 win whilst playing for Rotherham in a League Cup game against Notts County. I then played up front with Dave when I made my debut for Notts County in October 1967 at Meadow Lane against Crewe. Dave scored the winning goal that evening in a 1-0 victory then left the club in December to join Rotherham. Tommy Docherty had taken over at Rotherham and saw Dave in a reserve match when Rotherham played Notts. Dave went to Rotherham in an exchange for Keith Pring who came to Notts County and that was it. We did not come up against each other until the game against Sunderland in 1973."

LES BRADD

JACKIE ASHURST

MICK McGIVEN

MICK McGIVEN

Played in both games for Sunderland against Notts.

Midfielder Mick McGiven may well have been part of the cup final team but for an injury sustained in the third round. He remembers, "I tore my cartilage in the replay. I got fit just before the cup final after [physio] Johnny Watters worked on me. I played at Orient on the Monday night of cup final week and I remember going into a sliding tackle and the impact of it jarred my knee but that was actually a good thing as it freed my knee.

" **I was hopping about immediately afterwards and I remember Bob Stokoe shouting, 'What's the matter with you? You're hopping around like a rabbit!' I'd been out for a while but I thought I just might have a chance of being the sub at Wembley but I didn't and the rest is history."**

JACKIE ASHURST

Played at Notts County

Defender Jackie Ashurst (No relation to Len) played at Notts County and came on as a sub in the fourth round tie with Reading. He remembers the Mighty Jim's save from Les Bradd at Meadow Lane and the experience of playing in front of Montgomery, "I'd actually been substituted before then and was in the dug-out but I remember it well. It was a fantastic save, absolutely brilliant. Jimmy Montgomery was hard to get past. Jim used to say to me, 'Go for the ball unless you hear me coming and if you do get out of the way!' If he didn't punch the ball he might punch your head!"

ELSEWHERE IN THE CUP

Not a vintage round for cup surprises. The season's biggest shock was still to come with Sunderland going on to win the cup. Fourth division Bradford beat second division Blackpool while second division Swindon knocked out top-flight Birmingham who had been semi-finalists the previous year. Arsenal had been in the last two finals and would have reached a third in successive seasons but for Sunderland beating them in the semi-final. On third round day they came close to elimination, needing an 87th-minute equaliser from Hebburn-born George Armstrong at home to Leicester City.

NEXT UP

The winners of the Sunderland v Notts County replay had been drawn at home to either Doncaster Rovers or Reading who were due to meet 24 hours after Sunderland had put the not into Notts. Their tie had been postponed on the Saturday but when they got underway Reading emerged as 2-0 victors meaning that they would come to Roker Park led by the legendary Charlie Hurley in Round Four. Had Rovers won through it would have been Hurley's 1964 promotion-winning teammate Brian Usher who would have had a Roker reunion.

73 @FIFTY

THE KING
MEETS
THE MESSIAH

ROUND 4

DATE: Saturday 3 February 1973

SUNDERLAND 1
Tueart 38

READING 1
Chappell 13

ATTENDANCE: 33,913

73@FIFTY

Bob Stokoe was yet to be dubbed 'The Messiah' but Charlie Hurley was undoubtedly 'The King'. Hurley - who would be crowned 'Player of the Century' later in the decade in the club's Centenary year of 1979 had left Sunderland in 1969 after over 400 games for the Lads.

Renowned as, 'The Greatest Centre-half the World Has Ever Seen' according to his terrace chant, the opportunity for Hurley to bring his Fourth Division team to Roker Park was heaven sent. "I couldn't believe the cup draw when we were given a tie at Roker, for me it was like a long lost son going home" Charlie told me for the book 'Sunderland: Match of My Life'.

Then known as the Biscuitmen rather than the Royals, Reading had already knocked out Gillingham, non-league Hayes and Doncaster Rovers. As they came to Sunderland for what was their 200th game in the FA Cup Hurley's men were 13th in their league. Unsurprisingly with Charlie in charge they were good defensively having conceded only 19 goals in their 26 league games - the tightest in the division despite their modest placing. They had only leaked one goal in their four FA Cup games while in the League Cup they had played Second Division promotion chasers Fulham and only conceded one goal in each of the three times they met.

Largely the reason for this was goalkeeper Steve Death. He had the blinder of blinders at Roker Park. I still rate it to be the best performance I have ever seen by a visiting goalkeeper at Sunderland - despite at 5'7" Death being the smallest goalkeeper in the Football League. After a single game for West Ham he spent the rest of his career at Reading, totalling 537 appearances for them. He was Reading Player of the Year four times including this season and the one after. Until Edwin van der Sar of Manchester United broke his record in 2009 Death held the record of going an incredible 1,074 minutes without conceding a league goal. Sadly Steve Death died of cancer in 2003 aged only 54. His performance in the FA Cup fourth round at Sunderland in 1973 will never be forgotten by those who witnessed it. Also on Reading's books at the time was a young Steve Hetzke who would later play for Sunderland although he didn't feature in the tie with the Lads.

As Reading came to Roker Stokoe's Sunderland were getting going. After losing to league leaders Burnley a few days after he took over, going into the Reading game Sunderland were unbeaten in seven games under their new boss. The most recent of these had been a 2-0 home win over Millwall memorable for two reasons. One, quirkily, was that pop singer Lulu did the half-time draw. The other more significantly was that it marked the only appearance of Sunderland's new centre-forward John Hughes - the brother of Billy. Unfortunately John was injured in the game and never played competitively again. As of the end of the 2021-22 season this match was the last in which two brothers played at the same time in the same game (Ricardo Gabbiadini once played in the same game as his brother Marco at Leeds in October 1989 but Ricardo came on as sub for Marco). "The injury happened in the first 15 minutes" remembered John Hughes. "I went up for a ball. I was facing the wrong way and as I tried to push off the knee just went. That was me. I played through the rest of the game but I could hardly run. I'd had a bad time at Crystal Palace with my knee and this was my first game but the knee just went.

"To be honest, at the time I never thought that I wouldn't play again. I didn't think like that but once I spoke to the surgeon and the specialist they said that was it. If I'd done it nowadays they could probably have fixed it. It was a very disappointing end to my career.

"I stayed in Sunderland for a wee while. My wife was still in London and she was making arrangements to move up so she was obviously devastated as well. It was just one of those things. I was only 29. I watched them all the time. I remember when they won the cup.

"They were 750 to one and my wife said, 'Why don't you put a tenner on them?' but I said, 'Don't be stupid!' I should have listened to her especially as they were good enough to beat Arsenal as well, and Manchester City."

Perhaps John Hughes' injury was a blessing for Sunderland. It is unlikely Vic Halom would have been signed but for that injury. Halom would go on to play a key role in the cup run scoring a couple of very important goals as well as leading the line magnificently. Moreover John Hughes wouldn't have been able to play in the cup run even if fit. He was cup-tied having played for Crystal Palace in the third round against Southampton.

THE GAME

The 'Football' Echo headline told the story of the match: 'Goalkeeper Death keeps Reading alive'. Steve Death was outstanding, making fabulous saves from John Lathan, Bobby Kerr, Dennis Tueart and Ian Porterfield in particular. The cup run was highlighted by Monty's miraculous double-save in the final but also his super saves in the semi-final and in the fifth round at Manchester City, but the Mighty Jim wasn't the only goalkeeper to excel as Sunderland became cup winners.

Death deserved his bit of luck when a linesman's flag ruled out a last-minute 'goal' netted by John Lathan who had come in at centre-forward in place of the injured John Hughes. This was Stokoe's solitary change from the previous week's league victory over Millwall. Stokoe's popularity was building but it hadn't yet reached the levels of worship that would come. In this match he had to take a back seat in the popularity stakes to visiting manager Charlie Hurley who as expected was greeted like the returning hero he was.

Death had already made three good saves before Reading took a 13th-minute lead. The goal came from a Roker End corner with Les Chappell meeting Gordon Cumming's flag kick at the near post and scoring with a header.

Sunderland's response crashed on the rock of the goalkeeper who denied a long-range shot from Porterfield that had the diminutive keeper at full strength. Death was finally beaten seven minutes before half-time when Dennis Tueart equalised after good work from Lathan and Billy Hughes. It was just as well Tueart found the gap as no matter what else was thrown at him Death was almost unbeatable - and when he was beaten either the linesman's flag or the crossbar came to his rescue - Dick Malone seeing a shot come back off the underside of the bar early in the second half.

73 @FIFTY

TOP, L TO R:
DICK MALONE,
MICKY HORSWILL,
KEITH COLEMAN,
IAN PORTERFIELD,
JACKIE ASHURST,
JOE BOLTON AND
DAVID YOUNG

But for that equaliser maybe the cup run would have ended in a damp squib of a home defeat by a fourth division side.

Tueart was next to be thwarted by the goalie and the pressure increased even further when Sunderland had to use their one substitute to replace injured midfielder Kerr 13 minutes from time. Twelfth man Jackie Ashurst went into defence with Dave Watson switched to centre-forward and Lathan filling in for skipper Kerr. Tueart again was denied by Death and then in the dying seconds came the moment when only an offside decision stopped Lathan from adding his name to the list of cup run goalscorers. In the final analysis all 17 goals of the cup run were scored by people who played in the final.

The gate receipts of £15,650 were a new record for Roker Park but it was a record that wouldn't last long. The next two cup ties at Roker would bring crowds of over 50,000.

SUNDERLAND: Montgomery, Malone, Guthrie, Horswill, Watson, Young, Kerr (Ashurst 77), Hughes, Lathan, Porterfield, Tueart.

READING: Death, Dixon, Youlden, Wagstaff T (Butler 54), Hulme, Wagstaff B, Cumming, Chappell, Bell, Hunt, Habbin.

REFEREE: M E Jolly (Manchester).

ROUND 4 REPLAY

DATE: Wednesday 7 February 1973

READING 1
Cumming 78 (Pen)

SUNDERLAND 3
Watson 2, Tueart 14, Kerr 29

ATTENDANCE: 19,793

Charlie Hurley's programme notes regretted the injury to Tony Wagstaff who he felt had been "causing all sorts of trouble to Sunderland's right flank" while his praise for his goalkeeper was restricted to, "With Steve Death playing his usual game, which we all know is a regular game for him, Sunderland could not score."

Totally focussed on his own club as he made his way in management there was no mention of his own reception at Roker Park or even a welcome to his old club and its supporters - although Charlie loves Sunderland as much as Sunderland loves him. Nonetheless, elsewhere in the Reading programme it was noted that, "The Roker Roar shook the stadium."

Reading went into the replay as the last surviving Fourth Division team in the competition as they looked to reach the fifth round for the first time since 1935. Cup fever had hit the town. The crowd of just under 20,000 that squeezed in was almost double their previous highest of the season. That had been for their third round tie with Doncaster Rovers while in the league their highest home gate of the season so far was under five and a half thousand.

A group of Sunderland's reserve team players including Matt Robson and Ian Harrison had made their way to Reading to support the first team in their replay after playing games at Hull and Middlesbrough. Also lending his support was 1969 FA Youth Cup winner Fred McIver. He flew in from Belgium where he was playing for Racing Jets after being given a free transfer by Sunderland the previous summer.

Stokoe decided to get at Reading from the start. He had seen how Dave Watson had caused them problems at centre-forward in the latter stages at Roker Park. This resulted in Ritchie Pitt being brought in for his first FA Cup tie of the season although as Ritchie explains in this chapter he was far from thrilled about it.

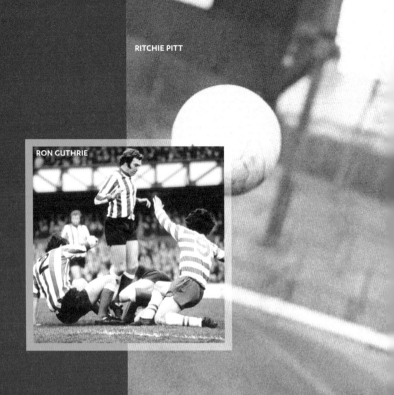

RITCHIE PITT

RON GUTHRIE

The manager's decision to play Watson up front paid immediate dividends. After all of Reading's resistance at Roker only 80 seconds of the replay had elapsed when Watson gave Sunderland the lead for the first time in the tie. Tueart started it by winning possession. He traded passes with Kerr and fired in a fierce shot. Having beaten the goalkeeper who had impressed so much there was disappointment when defender John Hulme managed to clear it off the line but Watson picked up the clearance on the edge of the box and rammed the ball into the back of the net.

David Young would collect a medal as unused sub in the final. He was also on the bench for the famous fifth-round replay with Manchester City but the only two games David played were two matches with Reading. A minute before Sunderland doubled their lead Young made a strong and successful tackle on first game scorer Chappell that had the home fans screaming unsuccessfully for a penalty.

Reading would get a penalty later in the game - the only one in the cup run - but by then the tie would be effectively over. Tueart doubled Sunderland's lead with a typically stylish goal. His approach play having led to Watson's goal, Tueart benefited from Watson's pass. As Dennis bore down on goal, Death rushed out as defenders Will Dixon and Brian Carnaby converged on him. Always quick thinking, Tueart reacted instantly, chipping the ball into a gaping goal.

Death was still difficult to beat and did well to prevent a Billy Hughes header from a corner extending the lead but Sunderland scored again before the half-hour mark. Once again Tueart and Watson were at the heart of it. Watson won a header to find Tueart who teed up Bobby Kerr to score what was the captain's only goal of the cup run. Four minutes later Bobby nearly scored again when he hit the bar, yet again after future England internationals Watson and Tueart combined. Tueart was later denied what would have been his third goal of the tie by another stunning Death save.

Spirited Reading did try to get back into the game. Young was booked for a foul on dangerman Chappell before Pitt brought down the same player for a penalty converted by Cumming 12 minutes from time. As Reading got up a head of steam Stokoe switched Watson back into defence to bolster the back line as Sunderland progressed to a glamour tie at Manchester City who won their replay with Liverpool on the same evening. Stokoe had left nothing to chance at Reading. Just as his first action as Sunderland manager had been to restore the traditional black shorts, he again turned his attention to the kit.

MICKY HORSWILL

73
@FIFTY

Declaring himself unhappy with the contrast of Sunderland's red and white stripes and Reading's blue and white hoops in the initial meeting at Roker Park, Stokoe had Sunderland kitted out in all-red for the replay.

READING: Death, Dixon, Youlden, Carnaby (Butler 70), Hulme, Wagstaff, Cumming, Chappell, Bell, Hunt, Habbin.

SUNDERLAND: Montgomery, Malone, Guthrie, Horswill, Pitt, Young, Hughes, Kerr, Watson, Porterfield, Tueart. Sub: Coleman.

REFEREE: Mr E Jolly (Manchester).

RITCHIE PITT

Played in the last six of the nine games it took to win the cup.

Ritchie Pitt was a hero of the cup final. He came into the cup team for the replay at Reading and from then on played every minute of the cup run but as he explains that didn't seem likely. New manager Bob Stokoe had signed the experienced David Young in Ritchie's position and was about to send Pitt and fellow young player Keith Coleman on loan to Arsenal. Left back Coleman had seen Stokoe bring in Ron Guthrie in his position.

"The night we played Reading in a replay that was the night Keith Coleman and I went on loan to Arsenal. When we got to Reading Keith and I stayed on the bus as the rest of the team got off. I got off later and walked into the ground. There was nobody in the dressing room so Keith and I went and stood in the centre circle as the rest of the team were in the penalty area.

Stokoe came up to us and said to me, 'Where's your boots? 'Mine are on the bus as I'm going off to Arsenal after the match' I told him. Stokoe said, 'You'd better go and get them 'cos you're playing'. I said, 'But I haven't trained with the first team for weeks'. 'That doesn't matter' he replied, 'You're playing.' 'Why am I playing?' I asked. 'Because I want to cup tie you before you go to Arsenal.' 'That will tell you what the relationship was like between me and the manager.

[Arsenal manager] Bertie Mee's assistant was at the match and afterwards took Keith and I down to London and put us into a hotel. I remember walking up the marble staircase at Highbury to the manager's office. At Sunderland I was on £40 a week and Keith was on £25 a week.

Straight away Bertie Mee said he was interested in signing us if we did well. He said the first thing he was going to do was double our wages to London rates so I was on £80 and Keith was on £50. I spoke up and said I thought we should both be on the same. He agreed and fortunately put us both on £80 not £50, so Keith was over the moon having gone from £25 a week to £80!"

Pitt actually partnered Young in the centre of defence at Reading as Dave Watson was switched from centre-half to centre-forward for the match. Before joining Pitt on loan at Arsenal Keith Coleman was named on the bench in the replay at Reading. While he didn't come on it was his only connection with the cup run.

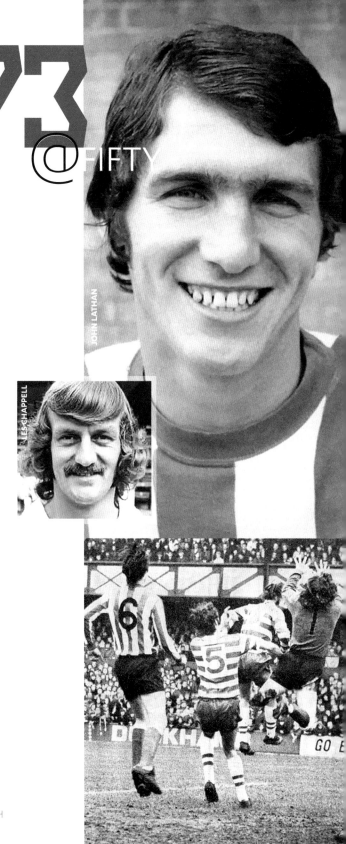

JOHN LATHAN

LES CHAPPELL

73 @FIFTY

JOHN LATHAN

Had a 'goal' disallowed at Roker

John Lathan started the home game with Reading at centre-forward having come off the bench in the third round replay against Notts County, "I remember playing against Reading. I remember 'scoring' in that game only for it to be given offside. The Reading goalkeeper Steve Death had a blinder that day, he was unbelievable. I thought I'd scored only to see the linesman's flag up".

VIC HALOM

Signed for Sunderland on the night of the replay at Reading.

Vic Halom would score one of the greatest goals in Sunderland's history in the next round against Manchester City as well as opening the scoring in the semi-final. He was the last piece in the cup-winning jig-saw and signed for Bob Stokoe following the replay at Reading, "I met him at Reading football ground immediately after the replay in the Cup. Basically Bob's pitch was that they were sixth off bottom in the league but had signed a few players and were still in the Cup."

LES CHAPPELL

Scored for Reading at Roker Park.

"I scored from a corner at Roker Park. I'd played with Dave Watson at Rotherham in 1965 and since then I'd played against him for Reading against Rotherham a couple of times and I'd scored on both occasions! When he first came to Rotherham as a youngster he came to live with me and my mum and dad as a lodger so I knew everything about him and how he played. He went on to have a fantastic career of course.

"At Roker Park Sunderland were the better side. We didn't have that many chances but I managed to score with a glancing header from a corner. Steve Death wasn't very tall but he was an excellent goalkeeper and he was outstanding at Sunderland. That wasn't a flash in the pan, he was consistently good. When Sunderland knocked us out we weren't expecting Sunderland to go on and win the cup so the manager deserves a pat on the back for that."

GORDON CUMMING

Scored for Reading in the replay.

"I'd played against Sunderland in the FA Youth Cup final for Arsenal in 1966 and loved playing in front of a big crowd at Roker Park for Reading when Les Chappell scored from my corner, The big thing that day was, 'The Charlie Hurley Show' because the place erupted when he came out. In the replay Sunderland were just too good for us and got ahead early on but at least I got a goal from the penalty spot. We never thought at the time that we had gone out to the winners but as the season went on we saw how sensationally Sunderland did."

VIC HALOM

DOUG WEATHERALL

journalist who was very close to the events at Sunderland.

"When Bob Stokoe was appointed - Sunderland were in deep Second Division relegation trouble, remember - I told him I hoped he won a couple of FA Cup ties 'and the place would take off.'

From his later years as a Newcastle player Bob and I were good friends. I recall with affection my late wife and I dining with him and Jean in the Lake District. I so wanted the best for him. But, of course, who could have even dreamed of what was to happen? He was the top Sunderland manager in my 90 years."

ELSEWHERE IN THE CUP

Five first division sides were knocked out by second division opposition. Newcastle were beaten at home by Luton Town who Sunderland would go on to meet in the quarter-finals. Former Manchester United winger John Aston did the damage at St James' with both goals in a 2-0 win for the Hatters. Millwall beat Everton 2-0 at Goodison Park. West Ham were knocked out at Hull and Carlisle beat Sheffield United 2-1 at Brunton Park.

While it took two replays Sheffield Wednesday eventually defeated Crystal Palace at Villa Park with a hat-trick from Brian Joicey who had scored at Wembley for North Shields as they won the FA Amateur Cup in 1969. Leeds didn't have it easy against third division Plymouth Argyle, edging past the men from the south-west 2-1 at Elland Road.

Only three of the 16 fourth-round ties pulled in crowds of under 30,000 with the biggest of the day being the 56,296 who packed Anfield for a goalless draw with Manchester City.

NEXT UP

The draw for the fifth round gave the winners of the Sunderland v Reading tie the toughest of tasks away to the winners of the Liverpool v Manchester City replay. Liverpool would go on to win the league and the UEFA Cup in 1972-73 but having just missed out on the league title with Manchester City the year before - both being a point behind Brian Clough's champions Derby - just under 50,000 saw City win their replay 2-0 and clear the way to what they thought would be an untroubled route to the quarter-final and beyond.

MATCH
OF THE
CENTURY

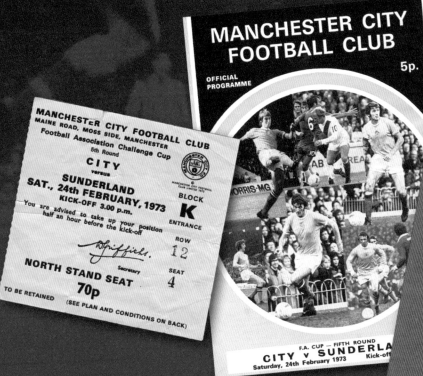

MANCHESTER CITY
FOOTBALL CLUB

OFFICIAL
PROGRAMME   5p.

ROKER
REVIEW

Sunderland v Manchester C. Tuesday, 27th February, 1973

6p VOL 2

F.A. CUP - FIFTH ROUND
CITY v SUNDERLA
Saturday, 24th February 1973   Kick-off

MANCHESTER CITY FOOTBALL CLUB
MAINE ROAD, MOSS SIDE, MANCHESTER

Football Association Challenge Cup
5th Round

CITY
versus
SUNDERLAND

SAT., 24th FEBRUARY, 1973
KICK-OFF 3.00 p.m.

You are advised to take up your position
half an hour before the kick-off

W. Griffiths.
Secretary

NORTH STAND SEAT
70p

TO BE RETAINED   (SEE PLAN AND CONDITIONS ON BACK)

BLOCK
K
ENTRANCE

ROW
12

SEAT
4

ROUND 5

DATE: Saturday 24 February 1973

MANCHESTER CITY 2
Towers 16, Montgomery OG 72

SUNDERLAND 2
Horswill 36, Hughes 68

ATTENDANCE: 54,478

THIS PORTION TO BE RETAINED

Block H № 13638
Ground—Roker End
F.A. CUP 5th ROUND REPLAY
SUNDERLAND v.
MANCHESTER CITY
ROKER PARK GROUND, K.O. 7.30 p.m.
On TUESDAY, FEBRUARY 27th, 1973
Secretary.
ADMISSION 40p

Issued subject to Rules & Regulations of the F.A.

73

@FIFTY

When Roker Park closed in 1997 this fifth round replay was voted by fans as the 'Match of the Century'. It was a truly great game but for me the first match at City's Maine Road was arguably even more important. Normally the most optimistic of supporters, as I arrived in Manchester a few hours before kick-off an unusual dose of realism struck my young mind. I vividly remember getting off the Supporters' Association No 1 coach and thinking in all reality by the time I got back on it we would be out of the cup.

In fact when I boarded the bus for the journey back to Sunderland I felt we were unlucky to have had to settle for a draw. Sunderland had played brilliantly against the cup favourites on their own patch and to this day I feel that Monty was fouled for City's equaliser.

Speaking immediately after the Round Four replay at Reading Bob Stokoe had felt that Sunderland might have as many as 4,000 fans at Manchester. It turned out there were about four times that many. Two big banks of red and white provided the Roker Roar in stereo for the citizens of Manchester. Those massed ranks of red and white were bolstered by some fans of Manchester United who turned up as their league match with Crystal Palace had been postponed. (Had they not been in the cup Sunderland would have been at nearby Preston for a league game that afternoon).

Almost exactly a year earlier Sunderland had gone out of the FA Cup at Maine Road against City. Not Manchester City, but Cardiff City in a Fourth Round second replay after two 1-1 draws. The game was on a Wednesday afternoon due to a miners' strike that had led to floodlighting being banned. Over 39,000 had turned up at Roker Park on a Monday afternoon for the first replay with Cardiff but there were fewer than 9,000 at the neutral ground of Maine Road. I didn't so much 'doll off' school as I went to see the headteacher Mr Copland at Ryhope School and told him I wouldn't be there the next day, as come what may I was going to the match. Fair play to him, he just said to make sure I brought in a note saying I had a cold.

By the time I came away from Maine Road a year later, after the tie with Manchester City, I didn't so much have a cold as a fever. All of Sunderland caught it. It was called cup-fever. I'd never seen or felt anything like it. Although my first match as an eight-year-old was a fourth round FA Cup tie with Peterborough in 1967, watched by over 44,000, I was considered too young to go to the next round against Leeds. After a couple of years of being taken to matches now and then I started going to every match a few weeks before the Lads were relegated in 1970. Since then I'd been one of those who never missed a game when crowds were regularly down to around ten or eleven thousand. Invariably I went in the Roker End which could hold 23,000 on its own. Now there was the prospect I might not get in.

The words on the Stokoe statue quote Bob as saying, "I didn't bring the magic. It's always been here. I just came back to find it." He had rediscovered that magic even before the teams ran onto the Roker turf for the replay. From the moment the final whistle went at Maine Road, I and thousands of others were convinced that Sunderland's name was on the cup.

You may dismiss that as the foolish ramblings of a 15-year-old but look in the record books and you'll see that fairy-tale or not, this one came true.

A year earlier in that second replay Monty hadn't played through injury and Sunderland had lost tamely 3-1 when the prize in the next round was a home tie with Leeds. This time Leeds would lie in wait again but not until Wembley and there was a lot of excitement to come before then!

THE GAME

With Vic Halom having been signed since the last round, for the first time in the cup run the eleven who would play in the final lined up together. Had David Young been fit he may well have played instead of Pitt but Pitt did so well - having been recalled from his loan to Arsenal - that he made it impossible to drop him for the rest of the run.

Having taken replays to dispose of third and fourth division opposition so far, the prospect of facing Manchester City at Maine Road was an entirely different proposition but since Stokoe's arrival the sleeping giant of Sunderland had been stirring. Seven days earlier promotion hopefuls Middlesbrough had been beaten 4-0 at Roker Park and so Sunderland set off for Manchester with a hungry and increasingly confident set of players eager to make a point.

Nonetheless City started as if they meant to swipe away the team from the lower reaches of the second division. Having seen off Liverpool in the previous round they had their eyes fixed on the quarter-final and beyond. Early on, Sunderland were under the cosh. City had the best of the first half an hour and took a 16th-minute lead through Tony Towers. City were good value for their lead and as the first half moved towards its closing stages it looked as if they were on course to cruise through to a comfortable victory.

The turning point came when Sunderland equalised nine minutes before the break. City's giant keeper Joe Corrigan was awarded a free-kick when Dennis Tueart challenged a bit too heartily for the referee's liking when Corrigan fumbled a ball.

As City tried to play their way out Micky Horswill stepped into the lime-light. Reading what was going to happen he gained possession, deftly dinked the ball over left-back Willie Donachie and proceeded to smash the ball beyond Corrigan. Game on. Cue pandemonium in the stands. The Lads were on their way.

Sunderland hadn't lacked belief all afternoon but they hadn't had much of the ball. Now they had that extra zip as City suddenly realised it wasn't going to be a canter into round six. Come half-time it was City who were ready for the whistle to stem the red and white tide bearing down on them.

While Bob Stokoe probably didn't need to instruct his side to produce more of the same, within the City dressing room Joe Mercer and Malcolm Allison evidently made it clear that their side needed to up their game and demonstrate their quality. Subsequently, the second half was a superb football match. Both teams attacked with verve. City brought numerous spectacular saves out of 'The Mighty Jim' who in particular thwarted Franny Lee and Mike Doyle.

DAVE WATSON

FIND THE BALL— PAGE 7

No. 31,542 (100th YEAR)

Echo
SUNDERLAND

SPORTS EDITION

SATURDAY, FEBRUARY 24, 1973   1p

City player ordered off in Cup thriller

Manchester City - - 2   Sunderland - - - - 2

WITH the Old Trafford game being called off, there were extra claims upon accommodation at Maine Road.
Sunderland took...

The goal that put Sunderland ahead was one of the best goals I have ever seen Sunderland score. It is what I call my dentist's goal. It's the goal I run through my mind over and over again whenever I have to visit the dentist and take my mind off what the medics are doing! Sunderland were such an exciting side at this time and so much of this excitement hinged on the pace of Tueart and Hughes. Both scored many brilliant goals and as a pair they dove-tailed beautifully. This goal was a classic of their combination play. Dennis the menace got the ball, promptly sending his mate on his way. Hughesy still had plenty to do but there was no stopping him. Billy turned Derek Jeffries inside out, cut inside and powered the ball past Corrigan. A truly great goal.

Sunderland didn't get the chance to settle on the lead. Within four minutes City were level, albeit in fortunate circumstances from a corner. These days if a forward gives a goalie a dirty look you expect a free-kick to be given. This though was 1973 and the officials deemed the pressure Montgomery was put under by Rodney Marsh to be fair. That night's 'Football' Echo gave the goal to Mike Summerbee direct from a corner although later it was harshly attributed as a Montgomery own-goal.

Both sides had chances to win the tie at the first time of asking but last ditch defending and good goalkeeping ensured a replay. There was though still time for another major talking point when City scorer Tony Towers was sent off. In a tetchy game which saw Porterfield, Horswill and Pitt booked, Towers was dismissed for an 83rd minute for an altercation with Horswill which also resulted in the Sunderland man's caution. Towers had been booked earlier for a foul on Halom, as had Tony Book for a foul on Bobby Kerr.

MANCHESTER CITY: Corrigan, Book, Donachie, Doyle (Mellor 74), Booth, Jeffries, Summerbee, Bell, Marsh, Lee, Towers.

SUNDERLAND: Montgomery, Malone, Guthrie, Horswill, Watson, Pitt, Kerr, Hughes, Halom, Porterfield, Tueart. Sub: Chambers.

REFEREE: Mr R Tinkler (Boston).

MONTY GATHERS

BILLY HUGHES FIRES PAST WILLIE DONACHIE

ROUND 5 REPLAY

DATE: Tuesday 27 February 1973

SUNDERLAND 3
Halom 15, Hughes 26 & 78

MANCHESTER CITY 1
Lee 53

ATTENDANCE: 51,782

Voted the 'Match of the Century' by supporters when Roker Park closed after 99 years in 1997, this replay with Manchester City featured the best Sunderland display I saw in the thirty years I attended Roker Park from 1967. Goodness knows how long it was before that since Sunderland produced a Wearside display to match this one.

Given the calibre of the opposition I'd venture to suggest it might have been the 1953 or 1935 visits of Arsenal. Reigning champions on both occasions, The Gunners were thrashed 7-1 in the fifties and beaten 5-4 in the thirties in a classic as Sunderland were en-route to ending their three year dominance as champions. Cup wins over Arsenal in 1961 or reigning champions Everton in 1963 could be other candidates. Some supporters might point to the 1961 FA Cup quarter-final with Spurs or the quarter-final replay with Manchester United three years to the day later but tremendous as those tussles were, they were drawn.

Sunderland didn't just win this pulsating replay with City, they deserved to. It was a match where they needed every last drop of effort and conviction to stave off a City fight-back as the Roker Roar at its loudest helped to carry the Lads over the line.

As in the first game at City's Maine Road the referee was Ray Tinkler of Boston. He had refereed the first two of the three-game fifth round epic with Leeds in 1967. There had been some fierce goings on in those games but the official kept a tight rein on what threatened to become an overly physical contest in this Roker replay. City were not just a side of supremely talented footballers. They had a steely side too. This was an essential requirement for any successful team in an era when players such as Chelsea's 'Chopper' Harris, Liverpool's Tommy Smith and Leeds' Norman 'Bites Yer Legs' Hunter were amongst the most high profile hard men in the game. Sunderland were no shrinking violets either - as Ritchie Pitt demonstrated in the opening moments of the final, but more of that later.

Cup fever had reached boiling point even before kick-off. Long before the turnstiles opened fans were milling around the ground, although there was frustration in Manchester where the cancellation of a football special train left many of their supporters struggling to make the journey. Even when City scored in the game their supporters could barely be heard but on this night of nights they could have had their full allocation or doubled it and been unable to make any impression on the white hot Wearside atmosphere.

For the replay Sunderland were unchanged from the first game four days earlier but City were missing right-winger Mike Summerbee, father of future Sunderland winger Nick. In his place came Ian Mellor (himself the father of future Liverpool striker Neil Mellor). Also in the City starting line-up was Tony Towers, not yet suspended despite his dismissal in the initial meeting.

The crowd of almost 52,000 produced record receipts of £26,048, an indication of the vast football inflation of the last half century. Even at modern day prices those fans would have had value for every penny. Bursting with confidence after their display at City and just one defeat in 12 since Bob Stokoe's first game, Sunderland tore into their illustrious visitors.

Three years earlier the FIFA World Cup final had seen arguably the greatest World Cup team of all - Brazil of 1970 vintage - destroy Italy 4-1 in the final. The best goal of that game was virtually re-enacted by Sunderland just 15 minutes into this replay. Whereas in Mexico in 1970 Jairzinho had worked the ball from the left side of the box to Pele who laid it off perfectly into the path of the onrushing Carlos Alberto who smashed the ball home right footed from the angle of the penalty area, at Roker Park it was Billy Hughes who found Ian Porterfield. Porter carried the ball along the edge of the box before involving the two other members of his midfield triangle. Finding Micky Horswill, the lad from Annfield Plain fed Bobby Kerr who laid the ball off, as had Pele for Brazil.

On the end of Kerr's pass was Vic Halom. This was only his fourth game for Sunderland but after this moment even if he had never played again Halom's name would have been indelibly etched in red and white folklore. Meeting the ball first time Halom leathered it in off the far post and into the back of the net.

It was the kind of goal that dreams are made of. It put Sunderland 1-0 up and it rocked the City aristocrats. Coming to a team 17th in the second division and just two points above a relegation place they felt that having failed to win at home they were going to make class tell in the replay.

However by the time of the goal they were already rocking. Mike Doyle had already been booked for a scything challenge on Hughes and nothing had prepared them for the crowd. Making the sort of din heard in the noisiest parts of the shipyards, the Roker Roar reverberated around the ground and far beyond. For all the fact that City had finished just a point off the top of the First Division the previous season and had knocked out league leaders Liverpool after a replay in the previous round, their away form was nothing to shout about.

At the time of their visit to Sunderland they had won only twice on the road whilst losing nine times as well as losing away to Valencia in the UEFA Cup and Bury in the League Cup. Faced with the rejuvenated red and whites in full flow they wilted before making a serious effort to claw their way back into the tie.

Just three minutes after scoring Halom almost netted again, future England keeper Joe Corrigan saving well after Halom's chance was created by Dave Watson heading down a Dick Malone free-kick.

VIC HALOM OPENS THE SCORING IN THE REPLAY WITH MANCHESTER CITY

BILLY HUGHES MAKES IT 2-0 V CITY

As City searched for an equaliser Jim Montgomery was called upon to save from Cold Heseldon born Colin Bell as well as Rodney Marsh, while Francis Lee was forced to shoot wide from a decent position under pressure from Ritchie Pitt.

Just 11 minutes after the first of the 'H-Bombers' put Sunderland ahead, Billy Hughes popped up with a goal that doubled the lead and put the Lads in total control. In the semi-final the second goal would be scored by Hughes from a Kerr throw after Halom had opened the scoring. It was the same here. Diminutive skipper Kerr had a long throw but deceived City, who were expecting it, with a shorter delivery from in front of the Main Stand as Sunderland attacked the Fulwell End.

Trading passes with Hughes the ball then broke kindly for Billy who showed typically quick feet to knock it into space before driving a shot as fierce as Halom's across Corrigan and into the far corner of the net.

Half time came and went with Sunderland 2-0 up. Everyone knew City would go for it in the second half and the next goal would be an important one. If Sunderland got it surely there would be no way back for the visitors but if it went City's way would the First Division side's momentum propel them back onto level terms?

Hughes was on a mission. This - and perhaps the following calendar year's game at Manchester United - was his best of many great games for Sunderland. Twice in the early stages of the second half Billy threatened while his big mate Horswill fired into the side-netting as Sunderland started positively. Then came the fight-back. Eight minutes of the second half had elapsed when City regained a foot-hold in the tie. Doyle, Towers and Bell combined to create a chance for Lee to clinically finish from close range with the seventh FA Cup goal of his City career.

In the third round at Notts County Sunderland had looked like losing. In the fourth round at home to Reading Sunderland had trailed to a side with an inspired keeper. The Lads had overcome these challenges but now this was an altogether tougher task. While they still led 2-1, an enormous amount of effort had gone into establishing that now halved lead, and this on the back of the weekend's exertions. There were 37 minutes for City to find an equaliser and force extra-time. Boosted by their goal City would come at Sunderland.

Hughes threatened again as the home team tried to respond but soon wave after wave of blue City shirts were besieging Monty's Fulwell End goal. There were 25 minutes between City's goal and the restoration of the two-goal cushion. During this spell Sunderland needed to be resolute. The back four rarely enjoyed the glory but it was in spells such as this that they did their work as well as the headline-makers. It wasn't just the defence of course, rather the whole team, but Messrs Malone, Watson, Pitt and Guthrie should take a bow for their contribution.

With Colin Bell increasingly influential, Mellor, Bell himself, Lee and Marsh all threatened an equaliser. The flamboyant Marsh came in for plenty of abuse from the crowd with a ditty that was re-used in the semi-final and final to the detriment of Charlie George and Allan Clarke with just the name changed but the wording is perhaps unsuitable for repetition here!

Sunderland defended heroically with sporadic attacks. There were 12 minutes left when the wind was taken out of City's sails as Hughes scored again. As with the opening goal it came from a fine passing move typical of the quality of the team. Having gained possession Porterfield played in the marauding Malone. He in turn found Halom who squeezed through a deceptively cute short pass to Tueart. Corrigan could only parry his future teammate's menacing shot.

The chance was far from gone though as both players racing to latch onto the rebound at the far post were in red and white shirts. Hughes got there before skipper Kerr to score his second of the night and make it 3-1. Billy could easily have had a hat-trick on the night as he also saw a header come back off the post.

Two minutes after Hughes made it 3-1 City defender Willie Donachie went into the book for dissent. Three minutes after that the referee also had to write down Marsh's name after his patience snapped with Horswill who had barely given him a kick all night and so Marsh exacted his own revenge. The youngest member of Sunderland's cup-winning team Horswill would do a similar nullifying job on Alan Ball in the semi-final and cancel out much of the influence of Billy Bremner and Johnny Giles in the final.

Although City kept looking to get back into the game, once Hughes had made it 3-1 there was negligible likelihood of them coming back as their near neighbours United had when 3-1 down late on in the 1964 quarter-final. Monty played in both of these games and come the final whistle he could join in with the elation of everyone in the ground. In fewer than three months since taking over a side struggling at the wrong end of Division Two Bob Stokoe had transformed Sunderland and taken the to the quarter-finals of the FA Cup in sensational style.

This was an unforgettable evening. If you were there, all this chapter can do is prompt your memories. If it was before your time then rest assured that this was a night which shaped the modern history of SAFC. After the match City supremos Malcolm Allison and Tony Book came into the Sunderland dressing room to wish Sunderland success. That was a touch of class on a night when the whole Sunderland side were a class apart.

SUNDERLAND: Montgomery, Malone, Guthrie, Horswill, Watson, Pitt, Kerr, Hughes, Halom, Porterfield, Tueart. Sub: Chambers.

MANCHESTER CITY: Corrigan, Book, Donachie, Doyle, Booth, Jeffries, Mellor, Bell, Marsh, Lee, Towers. Sub: Barrett.

REFEREE: Mr R Tinkler (Boston).

VIC HALOM

Scored the most spectacular goal of the cup run in the City replay.

" When that one went in, it just lifted. I'd really tonked it. Joe Corrigan was in goal for Man City, and to this day if I ever see him he always greets me with, 'Not you again'."

VIC HALOM

BILLY HUGHES WORRIES CITY GOALKEEPER JOE CORRIGAN

RITCHIE PITT

RITCHIE PITT

Spilled tears in the dressing room at Maine Road.

"The manager had signed David Young from Newcastle in my position and he was obviously itching to play David but when David got injured I was at Arsenal on loan. I'd played against Chelsea reserves on the Saturday and I got a phone call from Billy Elliott on the Sunday to say that David Young had been injured and they were recalling me from the loan and I would be in the first team squad for the next game against Middlesbrough.

I didn't really want to come back. I wanted to stay at Arsenal to be honest but then I played against Middlesbrough who we beat 4-0 and then the following week was Man City away. I was so pleased with the way I played at Maine Road I just sat in the changing room and I couldn't stop myself, I just cried for about 10 minutes."

"All the lads were coming up to me and asking, 'Are you okay? What's happened?' It was just sheer relief that I'd proved to myself and to the gaffer that I could play against the top teams and top players. It was a big moment for me. Franny Lee and Rodney Marsh were the two I was mainly in contact with but there was Mike Summerbee on the wing as well. They were all top players, probably one of the top teams in Europe."

MICK McGIVEN

Injured in the third round.

"I'd been in the dressing room for the Man City game. At that particular time Arthur Cox and Billy Elliott were running the team because Bob was suffering from migraine. I'm not sure how long it was but he was away from the club for around two weeks. He came back for the Man City game.

I was in the dressing room when he gave the team talk for the Man City game and Bob - Bless him - he was giving the team talk. Bob was monotone. It was the same tone all the time and he went on, and on, and on. All of a sudden the door burst open and there was [physio and former Celtic player] Johnny Watters with a greyhound and the tone of the dressing room just lifted completely as everyone burst out laughing!

Johnny was saying something like, 'He's called Sunny Day and he's in the seven o'clock at Boldon and he's a certainty!' Bob went mad and started shouting, 'What's going on? get that XXXXXXX dog out of here ' but by now everyone was laughing. He'd really lightened the atmosphere."

@FIFTY

TONY TOWERS

DICK MALONE

DICK MALONE

Played in all nine cup games.

"Mick McGiven's story about Johnny Watters and the greyhound is true - and for good measure Johnny came in wearing Vic Halom's platform soled shoes".

TONY TOWERS

Scored and was sent off for City in the initial tie.

"Every game in the FA Cup is a one-off game but when the opposition is Sunderland, with the supporters and everything it was a big occasion. I later came to play for Sunderland and had three and a half fantastic years up there. The people were great, just so down to earth. In the round before we played Sunderland we'd beaten Liverpool. We drew at Liverpool and won the home game but when we played Sunderland it was a frantic match."

"The tackling was furious and Micky [Horswill] was a bit of a biter. We had a bit of a tussle and I got sent off. I remember waiting in the tunnel for Micky as he was coming off just to say a few words to him but nothing transpired. The game itself flew by in a flash, it was so hectic."

"We knew the replay was going to be a hard game and we knew what the supporters were like at Sunderland. As we ran out of the tunnel the atmosphere was unbelievable. The Roker Roar was there and Sunderland deserved to win without a doubt. It was a one-off game, a cup game. The good thing about it from our point of view was the team that knocked us out went on to win the cup so there are no bad memories about that and the following year I signed for Sunderland in the deal that took Micky Horswill and Dennis Tueart to Manchester City. Before Sunderland won the cup they were struggling but the cup run pulled them out of it and the upsurge in the mood of the town did wonders for the local economy."

JIM MONTGOMERY

Made some spectacular saves at Maine Road but was harshly debited with an own goal.

"Rodney Marsh had a big influence on the equaliser at Maine Road. I remember that Micky Horswill was on the near post at the time. Micky stepped off the post and was about three or four yards out but the thing was I had never known Micky to be on the near post. I think if he hadn't been there I think I might have gone to either punch it or catch it further out. I didn't know if he was going to head it and that's why I stayed back. Consequently Rodney Marsh came in and sort of bundled me and the ball into the back of the net. I thought it should have been a free-kick but everyone has their own opinions.

"Manchester City had a fabulous team with Joe Corrigan, Colin Bell, Mike Summerbee and so on. To come away with a draw from their place was fantastic.

DRESSING ROOM CELEBRATIONS

JIM MONTGOMERY

73
@FIFTY

"I can remember Tony Towers being sent off having scored earlier with a shot low into my right hand corner. It was a great result for us and I can remember the feeling in the dressing room afterwards because we felt to get them back home in front of our crowd under the lights it would be something special.

"We always felt - especially in the later stages - that it was there for us to lose because we felt we could beat anyone. The atmosphere in the replay was incredible. It was right up there with the quarter-final replay against Manchester United in 1964 when we drew 2-2.

> "I always think the Manchester City replay was the game of the tournament. That defined Sunderland Football Club. It defined us."

"Billy Hughes was absolutely superb with the goals that he scored and of course Vic Halom's was a great goal. The atmosphere just lifted you. We knew that with that lot behind us we just couldn't let them down. They gave us an extra twenty per cent. After that game we had no doubt whatsoever that we could win the FA Cup!

"We always knew the crowd was a big influence for us and as the old saying goes the crowd were worth a goal start at Roker Park. The crowd were always fantastic."

ELSEWHERE IN THE CUP

Sunderland holding City in Manchester and then knocking them out was the only upset of the round. Elsewhere, the last Division Three outfit, Bolton, lost at home to Second Division Luton. Division Two sides Carlisle, Hull, QPR, Sheffield Wednesday and Millwall were all beaten by top-flight opposition while Leeds beat West Brom in the only all Division One clash.

On the same night as the City replay two of the players who had played in the earlier rounds - John Lathan and John Tones - weren't even at the match. They were playing for the reserves in a North Midlands League defeat at Scunthorpe where Bobby Kerr's brother George ran the show for the home side.

NEXT UP

By the time of the replay with City, both clubs knew that the prize was a home draw to second division Luton Town. Other than Sunderland they would be the only club left from outside of Division One. They had already won 2-0 in the league at Sunderland earlier in the season and were considered the plum draw.

The tie would be anything but easy but it was to come just two and a half weeks after the victory over City and Wearside couldn't wait.

HATTERS OFF

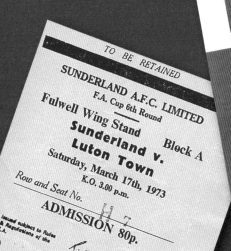

SUNDERLAND A.F.C. LIMITED
F.A. Cup 6th Round

TO BE RETAINED

Fulwell Wing Stand   Block A

Sunderland v. Luton Town

Saturday, March 17th, 1973
K.O. 3.00 p.m.

Row and Seat No.

ADMISSION 80p.

Issued subject to Rules
& Regulations of the
F.A.

Nº 445

SECRETARY

ROKER REVIEW

6p VOL 2

Sunderland v Luton Town, March 17th, 1973

F.A.CUP 6th ROUND

SUNDERLAND A.F.C. LIMITED, ROKER PARK G...

ROUND 6

DATE: Saturday 17 March 1973

SUNDERLAND 2
Watson 55, Guthrie 82

LUTON TOWN 0

ATTENDANCE: 53,151

FIND THE
BALL—SEE
PAGE 7

No. 31,560 (100th YEAR)

Watson g...
a tonic for
Roker men

Sunderland - - - 2   Luton Town - ...

IT WAS a gala occasion at Roker Park this afternoon...
capacity crowd packed in in good time to see Sunderl...
for a place in the semi-finals of the F.A. Cup in the...
round tie against Luton Town. Spectators had heeded...
warning to come early and...
there was a steady stream...
on to the terraces from...
12.30. For 20 minutes before the...
game there was the almost for-...
gotten spectacle of seeing...
uncomfortable spectators at the...
back of the Roker End being...
handed down over the heads of...
the crowd to the front.

BY ARG...

A little ceremony...
the game when Sunderl...
man Mr Keith Collings...
presentation to Jimm...
gomery to mark hi...
appearance, which was...
record in League and...

Manager Bob Stokoe m...
final selection dec...
naming David Young...

Luton Town made it...

SUNDERLAND
Montgomery
...Watson...

LUTON TOWN

TODAY'S RESULTS RO...

F.A. CUP—6th Rnd.

Chelsea ... 2 Arsenal ... 2

DIVISION II

Aston Villa 2 Portsmouth 0
...

73 @FIFTY

The quarter-final of the 1973 FA Cup run is something of a forgotten game. It is rather like the way in which the 1902 Division One win is the least known of Sunderland's six league titles, compared to the glamour of Raich Carter's class of 1936, The Team of All The Talents who took three titles in the 1890s and the Charlie Buchan side who reached the cup final as well as winning the league in 1913. When people look back at the FA Cup triumph of 1973 it is the victories over Leeds, Arsenal and Manchester City that are most talked about.

When Sunderland met Luton in the quarter-final the tie was between the only two teams left in the competition from outside the top-flight. It lacked the glamour of the fifth-round replay against star studded Manchester City but it dangled the carrot of a place in the semi-final. Such carrots are sometimes choked on. Think of the 2004 semi-final against fellow second tier outfit Millwall that offered not just a place in the final but almost guaranteed European football even if the final was lost (due to the final opponents qualification for the Champions League) or the 1976 quarter-final at home to Third Division Crystal Palace.

While the Luton tie attracts relatively little attention half a century on, that's not how it was at the time. With cup fever sweeping Wearside and all of County Durham the club had come up with the clever idea of issuing vouchers at the turnstiles at league games. These gave you a better chance of being able to obtain a cup ticket. So it was that a fortnight before the Hatters were due in town a crowd of 39,222 turned up for a league game with Oxford - the gate being a third higher than had witnessed the previous home league game against Middlesbrough, which in turn had been the biggest league attendance of the season so far.

A week before the home tie with Luton the Football Echo wrote, "No game has ever loomed quite so large on Sunderland's horizon as their FA Cup (sixth round) tie against Luton Town next week ...and none has received such undivided attention to the exclusion of practically every other topic." Such was the focus on the cup that on the same afternoon as these words were printed in the 'Football' Echo (such a sadly missed publication) there was a dress rehearsal for the cup quarter-final when Luton and Sunderland met in the league, this time at Luton's Kenilworth Road.

Despite Sunderland still being in relegation trouble (they were two points above the bottom two - only two went down - albeit with games in hand) and Luton still having a glimmer of a chance of promotion both teams made many changes for the league fixture as they rested players ahead of the cup clash. Stokoe made six changes with just Montgomery, Guthrie, Watson, Porterfield and Halom of the eventual cup final side playing, Halom being named captain against the club he had left the previous month.

Luton boss Harry Haslam became known as a wily and astute manager. He was in his first season as a Football League boss at the time and rested a quartet of his best players, particularly John Aston who had scored both goals as Luton had knocked out Newcastle at St James' in the fourth round. In a game where both teams evidently had their eyes on the cup-tie Luton deservedly won 1-0 with a goal scored by Don Shanks just before half-time.

The flu epidemic just after Stokoe took over, combined with a series of postponed league matches due to the cup run meant that Sunderland had a fixture pile-up. Sixteen games would be played in March and April - tough going ahead of the final for a small squad especially with league points still required to climb away from a danger area Sunderland were still in largely due to how few league games they had played.

So it was that just two days after their exertions in the quarter-final they had a league game at Preston. Moreover - in the days of just a single sub - it was an unchanged team Stokoe sent out to achieve a 3-1 win at Deepdale courtesy of some stout defending and goals from Halom and Hughes, who got two but worryingly had to go off injured late on.

THE GAME

This was the first tie of the cup run where a replay was not required. I'd not missed a home game since before the start of the decade, but not having a season ticket had to rely on the voucher system. So it was that I found myself with my dad in the Clock Stand Paddock rather than my regular haunt at the back of the Roker End. It gave the game a different perspective to my 15-year-old mind.

I was lower down than I usually was so couldn't see the pattern of play so well, but on the other hand I was half way up the pitch so could see the action at the Fulwell End better than normal. There was also the distraction of this slim person not far in front of me with lovely long blonde curly hair. It was only when the first goal came in the second half that as people went wild I saw that this girl of my dreams was actually a bloke. Maybe I'd managed to concentrate on the match more than I'd thought!

The game was preceded by a ceremony as Jim Montgomery received an award from chairman Keith Collings to mark Jim making more starts than anyone in the club's history, overtaking Len Ashurst. No doubt Monty would have rather been allowed to focus on the big game to come but it did not ruin his concentration as he promptly went out and kept a clean sheet. At the opposite end Keith Barber returned in goal for his first game in two months after injury.

Five months earlier Luton had comfortably beaten Sunderland 2-0 at Roker Park in front of a pre-Stokoe attendance of just over 13,000. As the sides took to the field for the cup tie that crowd had mushroomed to over 53,000.

Nine of Sunderland's side had been involved in the league fixture. These included Vic Halom, who on the first occasion was not only in the Hatters line-up but had scored the opening goal. The opening goal this time took a long time to come.

BOB STOKOE WATCHES DENNIS TUEART AND BILLY HUGHES IN TRAINING

Everyone knew the first goal was going to be crucial - especially as The Hatters were yet to concede a goal in the cup. Luton had done the double over Sunderland in the league and at that point of the season no-one had won more away games in the division than them. On the other hand, despite Sunderland's early season difficulties and the fact they were still in 16th position, at the time only league leaders QPR had lost fewer home games than the twice Sunderland's colours had been lowered at Roker. Indeed only ten goals had been conceded at home all season in the league, albeit two of them had been against Luton. So it was that the first half was a relatively cagey affair. Roared on by an expectant and excited crowd Sunderland pushed forward when they could but guided by the experienced Stokoe they weren't about to go gung-ho and allow the visitors to pick them off on the break.

Openings started to come with Halom, Tueart and Kerr having Sunderland's best first-half efforts whilst Monty had to show his bravery when diving amongst feet as Aston threatened a repeat of his St James' heroics. Sunderland had looked solid in the first half but so had Luton. If the visitors thought they could come out on top in the second half or take the Lads to yet another replay they were mistaken as Sunderland stepped it up from the word go after the break and Stokoe's team-talk.

Both goals in the 2-0 triumph would come from corners, just as the only goal of the final would. Captain Kerr took the first of these, driving over a cross that was met by the onrushing Dave Watson who eluded any attempts to mark him and bulleted home a header at the far post from inside the six yard box.

73

@FIFTY

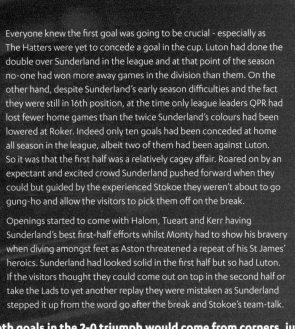

DAVE WATSON HEADS THE OPENING GOAL AGAINST LUTON

RON GUTHRIE MAKES IT
2-0 AGAINST THE HATTERS

73 @FIFTY

Now a goal behind, Luton came forward a little more only to find Sunderland's defence totally resolute - just as they had been when Manchester City threatened to get back into the game in the previous round. With the Hatters needing to score it also started to create a little more space for flying wide-men Hughes and Tueart to exploit. Although the game opened up the second goal also came from a set-piece.

As with the first goal the flag-kick was taken from the corner where the Main Stand met the Roker End but this time Hughes rather than Kerr was the taker. There was another difference too. Despite Watson scoring from an earlier corner this time it was Pitt who ventured forward from central defence. Judging the flight of the ball well, he met it just inside the penalty area and purposefully headed the ball into the danger area. Unnoticed by the Luton rear-guard who were primarily concerned with the towering Pitt and their former teammate Halom, left-back Ron Guthrie had sauntered casually into poacher's territory without being picked up.

As Pitt's header came to him the defender had his back to goal. A month short of his 29th birthday Guthrie had only ever scored twice in his career but chose this moment to channel his inner striker and acrobatically twist and perfectly volley home.

There were only eight minutes left. It was all over bar the shouting - which meant it was far from all over as Roker Park went crazy. Sunderland were destined for the semi-finals of the FA Cup. Most sadly in the half a century since this glorious day, the world's oldest football competition (the creation of Sunderland-born CW Alcock) has ridiculously been allowed to lose some of its sheen and glamour but make no mistake about it back in the day the FA Cup was not called THE Cup for nothing. This was the most prestigious knock-out trophy going, in the year after its Centenary final. Sunderland had only ever won it once and as everybody on Wearside kept repeating that was in 1937. This time those last two digits were the other way round and this was seen as an omen.

Moreover, The Wearsiders had not been in the semi-finals since the mid-fifties. Back then Sunderland were known as 'The Bank of England Club'. Full of the top stars of the day, Sunderland were the only club in the country to be able to boast that they had never played in anything but the top-flight since coming into the league. In stark contrast, in 1972-73 the club had endured a decade and a half of being decidedly in the doldrums.

A first relegation in 1958 on the back of suspensions and fines to the club, officials and players (after financial misdemeanours were exposed) had been followed by six long seasons in Division Two. Even after a 1964 promotion, six years back in Division One brought a high point of only 15th place before a second relegation in 1970 and a huge drop off in crowds as fans questioned the club's ambition.

Now Bob Stokoe had come along, taken Sunderland by the scruff of the neck and shaken it back to life. On the night Sunderland qualified for the semi-finals the clocks went forward to signal British Summertime. It was certainly the dawning of a new era for the club but many of the fans could have done without the loss of an hour overnight. There was beer to be drunk, songs to be sung - and the semi-final draw to come in two days' time!

SUNDERLAND: Montgomery, Malone, Guthrie, Horswill, Watson, Pitt, Kerr, Hughes, Halom, Porterfield, Tueart. Sub: Young.

LUTON TOWN: Barber, Ryan (John), Thomson, Shanks, Garner, Moore, Ryan (Jim), Anderson, Busby, Hindson, Aston (Hales 70).

REFEREE: Mr J Taylor (Wolverhampton) who refereed the following year's FIFA World Cup final.

ELSEWHERE IN THE CUP

Including Sunderland's tie with Luton, three of the quarter-finals produced a winner at the first time of asking. Wolves eased past Coventry 2-0 at Molineux, a Peter Lorimer goal saw Leeds beat Brian Clough's Derby at the Baseball Ground and Chelsea and Arsenal drew 2-2 at Stamford Bridge.

NEXT UP

The semi-final draw on the Monday lunchtime after Sunderland defeated Luton teased supporters by pairing The Lads with the only 'either/or' tie of the draw, being pitted against Arsenal or Chelsea. Wolves were the team supporters wanted. They would have been far from easy opposition as they were currently sixth in the top-flight. On the other hand Leeds were third in the table but with the games in hand to enable them to catch leaders Liverpool.

Had Chelsea managed to win at Highbury in their replay with Arsenal they might have been more attractive. They were 12th in the 22 team top-flight and had only won three league games away from Stamford Bridge. If they lost to Arsenal then Sunderland would face the team sitting second in the table, just two points off the top.

There wasn't long to wait to discover whether the Londoners in the semi-final would be of red or blue persuasion, The Gunners came through 2-1 on the night following the draw and all attention turned to the team from north London.

HORSWILL, PITT, PORTERFIELD AND HUGHES CELEBRATE WITH GUTHRIE (NO 3)

RON GUTHRIE

Scored in the quarter-final against Luton.

" I've got a DVD of the highlights of the game. I always used to go up for corners. I'd try to sneak up when Billy was taking the corner. I'd saunter up and get somewhere near the penalty spot. Nobody had told me to do it but I always did.

"Ritchie won the header from the corner and knocked it towards goal. I was about seven or eight yards out and managed to get a sort of bicycle kick over my head. My main job was helping to get clean sheets but getting a goal was a highlight. Winning the cup was the best thing but scoring a goal was good for me."

VIV BUSBY

Future Sunderland assistant manager who played for Luton Town at Roker Park.

"The crowd of 50,000 was incredible. The atmosphere was amazing, the crowd played a massive part for the Sunderland team. I know only too well, having later being assistant manager at Sunderland, how important the crowd is. I remember the top players for Sunderland such as Ron Guthrie, Dave Watson and my old friend Vic Halom.

During the game I don't think we had much possession and the quality of the Sunderland side was for all to see. We were beaten by a better side on the day. That's why they managed to win the FA Cup, a great manager in Bob Stokoe and great goal keeping by my old friend Jim Montgomery.

JIMMY HAMILTON

Sunderland's youngest ever goalscorer and on the fringe of the team in the cup-winning season.

"It was quite difficult. We made several changes for that league game at Luton and I do remember thinking before the match, 'If I get a hat-trick here I could be sub for the cup tie' but we lost 1-0 and I didn't have a good game. Generally as a team we got a bit of a drubbing football wise. I put a lot of work in and I was shattered, but having lost and not played well there was no chance of me being involved in the following week's quarter-final.

"The team in general struggled that day. Luton were the better team that afternoon but we went on to win the big game that mattered. I was very much to the side of things. I was just put in for that game because I was a goalscorer. My scoring record was good with the reserves but the cup-winning team was so good it was difficult to get into the team ahead of players of the calibre of Dennis Tueart and Billy Hughes."

MICKY HORSWILL

On his role in the team.

"The first thing Bob Stokoe did when he came to the club was to get us settled. He said, 'We are going to stop losing games!' The idea was that we'd start picking up points and then we'd start winning games. He disciplined me to sit and cover everybody. Everyone else got a free rein to go and do what they did. Players like Dennis and Billy had been ordered by Alan Brown to stay in certain areas of the pitch but they were given the freedom to roam wherever they wanted knowing we had someone in midfield that was sitting there to stop teams breaking on us.

"That was my job. Breaking things up was my strength. I wasn't a ball player I was the defensive player who loved stopping goals more than scoring goals even though I know that sounds stupid.

"When I first got into the team I was just a young kid and I was so pleased about it, I thought I could do anything. I could pass it or I could score and I thought I was the bees knees. We used to train at Washington and on an afternoon we sometimes used to go to a little greasy spoon café right in the middle of Washington where the bus station used to be and we'd have pie and chips or something.

"One day I went in and Ian Porterfield was there. I didn't speak much to the first-teamers because I was just a young kid but Ian asked me to come and sit beside him. He asked, 'Are you enjoying everything?' to which I said, "It's fantastic. It's all I ever wanted to do to play for Sunderland." He said to me...

We love having you in the team. If there is somebody needs sorting you go and sort them and you go and win the ball.' It was great to hear so I said, 'Thanks very much' and he continued. He said, 'Can I give you a piece of information, some advice?' I said 'Yes' and he went on, 'When you go and win the ball, give it to one of us that can play.' I thought he was kidding but he was serious.

"I wasn't someone who could create but I could stop other people playing. I thought of that for the rest of my career so I used to win it and give it to somebody else as quickly as I could. You need a blend of players. The best 11 individuals in the world would not be a team but we were. That's why Manchester City today have got people who between them can manage all aspects of the game and we were the same.

"We had Vic up front who we could hit. We had two really fast forwards in Dennis and Billy. We had me who was disciplined in midfield, we had Ian who was a great footballer and a creator, we had Bobby who was a workhorse and a back four who were all very powerful in the air and on the floor. Dave Watson was very quick and used to cover everybody at the back and the fella in goal wasn't bad either. I've seen him make better saves than he did in the cup final. We played at Fulham one time and he made a save that I've never seen anything like. We all trusted each other and that was a big part of our make-up."

73 @FIFTY

GUNNED DOWN

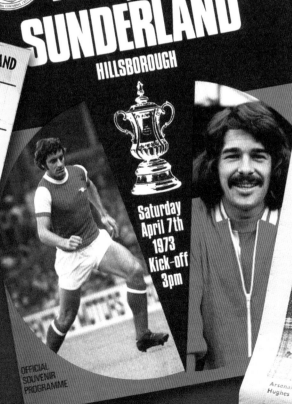

THE F.A. CUP SEMI-FINAL
ARSENAL
v
SUNDERLAND
HILLSBOROUGH

Saturday
April 7th
1973
Kick-off
3pm

OFFICIAL
SOUVENIR
PROGRAMME

SHEFFIELD WEDNESDAY F.C. LTD.
HILLSBOROUGH, SHEFFIELD

FOOTBALL ASSOCIATION CHALLENGE CUP

SEMI - FINAL
1973
Saturday, April 7th
KICK-OFF 3·0 p.m.

General Manager and Secretary

RESERVED SEAT £3·00

Issued subject to the Rules, Regulations and
Bye-Laws of the Football Association
No Tickets exchanged nor money refunded
THIS PORTION TO BE RETAINED

SOUTH STAND

ENTRANCE
J

GANGWAY
10

To the RIGHT

ROW
R

SEAT
165

YOU ARE REQUESTED TO
TAKE UP YOUR POSITION
THIRTY MINUTES BEFORE
KICK-OFF

SEMI-FINAL
Hillsborough

DATE: Saturday 7 April 1973

SUNDERLAND 2
Halom 19, Hughes 63

ARSENAL 1
George 84

ATTENDANCE: 55,000

FIND THE
BALL—SEE
PAGE 7

No. 31,578 (100th YEAR)

NEXT STO

Ha
pa

SUNDERL

THERE was a tre
welcome awaiting
derland team wh
arrived at Hillsbo
their F.A. Cup se
against Arsenal this
noon. All open
around the ground
thronged by supporters
most of them appeare
be pro-Sunderland. In
the ground the recep

BY ARGUS

Arsenal defender McNab bout Sunderland's
Hughes in this afternoon's F.A. Cup semi-final clash at
Hillborough

TODAY'S RESULTS ROU

F.A. CUP: Semi-Final
Arsenal   1   Sunderland 2
(Half-time)

DIVISION II
Bristol C

Leeds U.

Arsenal were bidding to become the first team to reach three successive Wembley FA Cup finals, and in turn become the first team to play in three consecutive FA Cup finals since Blackburn Rovers in the 1880s. Sunderland had only ever been to Wembley once before - in 1937 - and were still in the bottom half of the second division, albeit with games in hand.

In contrast The Gunners were in second place in the top-flight, just one point behind Liverpool. Two years earlier Bertie Mee's men had become only the second club of the century to achieve the elusive double of FA Cup and League title, while in 1972 they had lost the centenary final to Leeds United.

One memory that sticks in my mind from the pre-game build up at Hillsborough is the sight of an Arsenal fan wearing a hat covered in metal lapel badges of Arsenal. Despite the efforts of George Forster at the Supporters' Association in Sunderland there wouldn't have been enough different SAFC badges to cover the peak of a baseball cap. It seemed to indicate that Arsenal were used to the big-time that had escaped the Wearsiders for so long.

In an earlier era Sunderland and Arsenal had contested the top games in the land back in the thirties at a time of the likes of Raich Carter and Alex James. More recently in 1961 there had been a famous cup clash where two great goals from Stan Anderson gave Sunderland a victorious scoreline that would be repeated this time around.

Sunderland's cup side was by now settled. The same XI had been unchanged since the fifth round game at Manchester City but one of Sunderland's side could have been lining up for Arsenal. As explained in the section on the fourth round with Reading centre-back Ritchie Pitt (and Keith Coleman) had been on loan at Arsenal in the spring. Had Ritchie signed for the Gunners - and not been cup-tied bearing in mind Ritchie's earlier comments about Stokoe cup-tie-ing him before his loan - then perhaps he might have had an opportunity in the semi-final.

Arsenal were without centre-half Frank McLintock who had been injured in the previous week's game against Derby County. In his place they drafted in former Coventry centre-half Jeff Blockley. He had played at Wembley earlier in the season for England so was no mug, but was coming back from injury having not played since mid-February and was caught out for the crucial opening goal.

While Pitt's loan to Arsenal was curtailed when he came back to Sunderland and established himself in the team as a physically commanding defender (with fellow loanee Keith Coleman also returning), the Gunners interest in Sunderland's young players didn't end there. On the day of the semi-final Sunderland's solitary substitute was the elegantly creative midfielder Brian Chambers.

Brian was a sub three times during the cup run and was listed as twelfth man in the programme for the final (Rather than David Young who was the actual sub at Wembley) but never actually played a minute during the cup run. However he did play in the 1972-73 FA Cup - for Arsenal! With a transfer lined up before the final, Chambers was transferred to Arsenal during the summer.

Brian subsequently played for Arsenal in a match for third place in the FA Cup against fellow semi-final losers Wolves. Although this was for the 1972-73 FA Cup the game was held over to the start of the following season. On August 18 Chambers lined up alongside seven of the players who had faced Sunderland in a 3-1 defeat to Wolves at Highbury! These third and fourth place games took place between 1970 and '74.

While Chambers belatedly got to play in the 1972-73 FA Cup he had to settle for a watching brief in the semi-final as did the vast legions of the red and white army. Tickets had been like gold dust and many had to content themselves with listening to the radio to follow the match.

THE GAME

Both teams changed their strips as there was a colour clash. The Gunners donned a yellow kit such as they had worn when winning the cup in their double-winning season two years earlier. For Sunderland it was an all white strip which had been delivered to the team hotel in Buxton in the run up to the game. As the team travelled to the match from their Derbyshire base there was a lot of snow but fortunately none in Sheffield, so those white strips stood out.

A gate of 55,000 produced record semi-final receipts of £82,500. The crowd of course were bedecked in red and white but it was evident from the roars from the stands and the celebrations of the goals that the Wearsiders had managed to procure many more tickets than the Londoners, as well as being backed by the neutrals with tickets from the FA. Sunderland had been allocated the vast open kop (it was roofed in 1986) as well as their share of the seated areas.

As so often, Arsenal were aristocrats of the game. Their supporters may have taken their second division opponents lightly but it is unlikely that the players weren't fully prepared. They had seen Sunderland get the better of much fancied Manchester City over two games, dispose of Luton in the quarter-final and had seen their manager Bertie Mee recently pull in a couple of Sunderland players on loan, including of course Ritchie Pitt who would be one of the men blocking their path to Wembley.

Having won the toss Arsenal decided to start the game attacking the end housing their own fans. This gave Sunderland the chance to get on the front foot by attacking the end housing much of their support. A strong, blustery wind greeted the teams but it wasn't just the elements that blew Arsenal away.

As in all the big cup ties Sunderland's triumph was as a result of a gargantuan team effort but in this game in particular it was the 'H-bombers' of Halom and Hughes who did the damage. They got the goals and you can add Mick Horswill to the H's who harassed the life out of the men from Highbury.

It is a wonder that Horswill did not add to his goal at Manchester City in the semi-final or final. For a player whose main job was to nullify the creative geniuses who could unpick Sunderland's defence Horswill got in a lot of shots in at Hillsborough and Wembley.

73

**MONTY, HUGHES AND KERR
CONSIDER HOW THEY CAN SNOOKER ARSENAL**

CAPTAIN BOBBY KERR

LEFT TO RIGHT: JIM MONTGOMERY, JOE BOLTON, BOBBY KERR AND RITCHIE PITT ON THE GOLF COURSE

VIC HALOM SCORES THE
OPENING GOAL AGAINST ARSENAL

73

@FIFTY

Early on in the semi-final he drew a spectacular flying save from Bob Wilson and it was from his intelligent lofted ball over the top of the Arsenal defence that the opening goal came.

Nineteen minutes had gone when retreating Arsenal centre back Blockley tried to play Horswill's long ball back to his keeper Wilson. Throughout the cup run Sunderland's refusal to give up on anything became symbolic of their approach. Never was this truer than with this goal. Vic Halom had been breathing down Blockley's neck and chased the back pass.

Vic got to it a fraction before the keeper. Knocking it past the goalie Halom went on to bundle the ball into the empty net despite an awkward bounce. If anyone from Highbury doubted they were in a game, they knew now as Sunderland threatened to do to Arsenal what they had done to Manchester City.

England international Peter Storey was the hard man in Arsenal's side. Six minutes after his side went behind he went into the book for a foul on Billy Hughes, but Arsenal still had plenty to offer and with half an hour to play hit the base of the post through Hebburn-born former Newcastle junior George Armstrong, although Monty did have it covered.

Arsenal weren't the only ones to strike the woodwork. Soon afterwards the top of the bar was clipped by Hughes' in-swinging corner. Arsenal were struggling to cope with the physicality of goalscorer Halom who thrice more posed them serious problems in the first half, on one occasion seeing his effort hacked off the line. With a bit of luck Halom could have gone down in history as a Hillsborough hat-trick hero. Halom did get his name in the referee's book moments before break, for what the official described as, "Violence of the tongue".

Just before this the last major attack of an incident packed first half had seen Monty make one of his top three saves of the tournament - along with the famous double-save in the final and his miraculous stop from Notts County's Les Bradd in the third round. Once again it was Armstrong causing the problem. His shot from the angle of the box looked to be on its way to being a routine save until a deflection required 'The Mighty Jim' to somehow redirect himself after seeming to have put his weight into diving the other way. World Cup winner Alan Ball tried to get to the rebound but the ever alert Monty quickly knocked the ball away from Ball who had scored in Arsenal's last four FA Cup games.

Ten minutes after the break Arsenal withdrew the Halom-hounded Blockley and brought on John Radford. Many a Sunderland supporter had been delighted to learn that Radford wasn't starting. Deserving of many more than the two England caps he earned, in 2023 Radford remains Arsenal's youngest-ever hat-trick scorer having scored one when he was only 17. Seventeen was also the number of goals Radford had so far in the season. He was unquestionably a new and additional threat to a defence that was demonstrating the same resolute resistance that was characterizing the cup run as much as the free-flowing football of the front men.

Radford was immediately into the action, crossing for Charlie George who had two shots blocked. Defender Peter Simpson also fired in an effort but it was far from one-way traffic. Goalkeeper Wilson needed attention from the trainer after thwarting Hughes but the Gunners stopper soon had more to concern him when he conceded again.

Diminutive Bobby Kerr had strength that belied his size. This included his ability to deliver long throws and from such a delivery Tueart did well to flick it on for Hughes to apply a second header. Billy's effort looped beyond the despairing Wilson who got a hand to the ball but could only help it into the net as Sunderland doubled their lead.

On the only previous occasion Sunderland had qualified for the FA Cup final at Wembley the second goal in a 2-1 win against London opposition [Millwall] had come at the same stage with a header from a Scot, namely Patsy Gallacher scoring after 67 minutes while here Billy Hughes netted in the 63rd minute.

Sunderland were good value for their lead against the Gunners. Arsenal had threatened sporadically but had never been allowed to get into their stride. Now Sunderland led 2-0 but there was a third of the game still to play. Arsenal were a top quality team. They would finish second in the league that year - four points ahead of third placed Leeds - and with nothing to lose would use all their artillery against Stokoe's men.

Would the Wearsiders wilt? They had had to resist a Manchester City fightback when the fifth round opponents halved a 2-0 lead. Now with the prize of a place in the final tantalisingly near they would have to repel whatever Arsenal had to throw at them. The Lads had one foot in the final but would anyone put their foot in it? Everyone would be desperate not to make a mistake but such tension can lead to mistakes so while Sunderland were confident, and with good reason, there was a long way to go and nothing could be taken for granted.

Already cautioned, Peter Storey escaped a second punishment when he brought Hughes down five yards outside the box soon after Hughes' goal. Dick Malone was next in the book for pulling back Radford with 15 minutes to go. So far though it was not a case of Sunderland seeing out time.

Indeed they continued to threaten a third goal, Wilson being extended by Tueart and then having to react smartly to stop Hughes pouncing on the loose ball. Sunderland's attitude was attack was the best form of defence and the Gunners knew that the more they pushed men forward, as they must, the more chance Sunderland would score a third.

Tempers were becoming frayed with Ron Guthrie and Charlie George having their names taken after a clash before George made a more telling contribution when he pulled a goal back for Arsenal with six minutes to go, his shot on the turn having just enough power to squirm past Monty and trickle into the back of the net. The Arsenal scorer raced to retrieve the ball and re-start the game. To their credit Sunderland kept their nerve and did not panic in those closing moments.

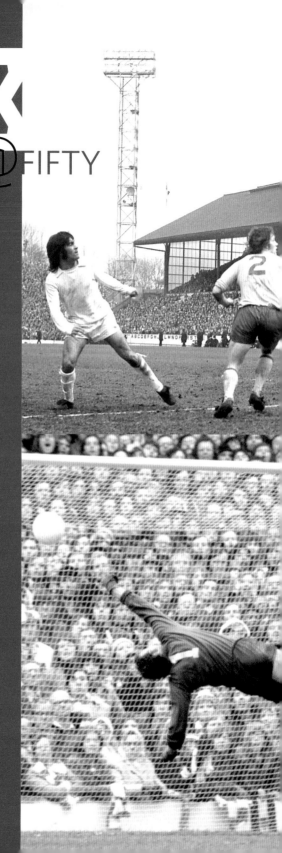

73
@FIFTY

BILLY HUGHES DOUBLED THE LEAD IN THE SEMI-FINAL

73@FIFTY

Despite - or perhaps because of - their lack of big game experience Sunderland played out the last few moments seemingly without fear although when referee Smith blew the final whistle as Arsenal were preparing to take a corner the feelings of elation were mixed with a moment of relief that the Gunners hadn't sneaked a late draw.

It took a few moments for the realisation to sink in that Sunderland had reached Wembley. Hardly any Sunderland supporters had ever been there but the Lads were on their way. Before then though there was the joy of insisting 'The Messiah' came back out to take the salute of the crowd. Nowadays it is routine for players and managers to acknowledge the crowd. We even have the regular occurrence of teams taking outstanding players off with a couple of minutes to go just so they can milk a personal ovation. In 1973 this was a rarity but those moments as Stokoe raised his arms to accept the thanks of the legions of SAFC supporters was a genuine highlight of the entire cup campaign.

A little over four months earlier Sunderland couldn't pull in 12,000 for a league game, now there would be tens upon tens of thousands clamouring for a ticket for the cup final. The town - Sunderland was still a town - was bouncing. A smile was on every face, people couldn't wait to get to work to talk football, productivity was blossoming massively and a few days later several of the team including all four Scots (Porterfield, Hughes, Kerr & Malone) joined Rod Stewart and the Faces on stage at 'The Mecca' (where the huge Tesco near the Stadium of Light now stands) in a gig which the celebrated Radio One DJ John Peel declared was the best he had ever been to in his life.

SUNDERLAND: Montgomery, Malone, Guthrie, Horswill, Watson, Pitt, Kerr, Hughes, Halom, Porterfield, Tueart. Sub: Chambers.

ARSENAL: Wilson, Rice, McNab, Storey, Blockley (Radford 55), Simpson, Armstrong, Ball, George, Kennedy, Kelly.

REFEREE: Mr D W Smith (Gloucestershire).

ELSEWHERE IN THE CUP

Just one other game of course, and just one goal settled it as Leeds captain Billy Bremner scored mid-way through the second half of the semi-final with Wolves at Manchester City's Maine Road. Leeds fielded nine of the side who would line up against Sunderland in the final. They were without the resolute Norman Hunter and mercurial winger Eddie Gray. World Cup winner Jack Charlton and Wembley substitute Terry Yorath came into the starting line-up although Big Jack had to come off before half-time after pulling a muscle.

NEXT UP

No need to huddle around a transistor radio for the cup draw. There were just two teams left standing: Sunderland and their fierce rivals Leeds United. The Wembley date was set for 5th May - almost an entire month in which cup fever on Wearside would explode.

73 @FIFTY

JIM MONTGOMERY

Played in every game of the cup run.

"I always remember Bally ruffling my hair after one particular save I made from George Armstrong, low down near the post after I'd had to change direction when the shot was deflected."

KAREN CRAVEN

Bob Stokoe's daughter

"For my dad his favourite game was the one against Arsenal. It was the manner of the win and the whole atmosphere as Sunderland reached the final when he came out of the dressing rooms to take the salute of the supporters."

LINDA HUGHES

Widow of winning goal scorer Billy Hughes

"The semi-final was a big, big favourite. The semi was 'It'. A supporter led us wives totally in song throughout the whole game. He had his back to the pitch and just led us so we just sang non-stop. The atmosphere was wonderful, and obviously playing Arsenal, crikey me! I got to know Charlie George later when Billy and Charlie were teammates at Derby although that was short-lived."

JEFF BLOCKLEY

Arsenal defender whose back-pass was cut out for Sunderland's opening goal of the semi-final.

"I dropped a back pass short to Bob Wilson. I don't know who it was that snuck in to knock it past Bob. I wasn't match fit. I'd been out for six weeks and it was my first game back but we had injuries and if you were told to play you played! Sunderland had their name on that cup. I got a lot of criticism for that moment but you just take it and what will be will be."

VIC HALOM

Scored the opening goal of the semi-final.

"We didn't just beat Man City or Arsenal - we took them apart. They were fabulous sides, and we dismantled them. I certainly knew that we would lift the cup. It's that little thing that you never say - but it was in there. Once we'd beaten City in the replay the rest was a formality. Some will say it was written, but there's a long way from it being written to actually getting there. There's a lot of hard work and sweat that still needs to go into it. We really did take Arsenal apart, which was no mean feat with the players they had. At Hillsborough in the semi-final we should have been three or four up at half time. I had two cleared off the line. We 'marmalised' them. It was no fluke. When Arsenal were a goal down at half time they were probably saying that we hadn't taken our chances. They thought we wouldn't have another half like that, but we did. There was a genuine belief that we could take the big side apart. I don't know whether they underestimated us or not, but we knew.

"For my goal Micky Horswill just lifted the ball on, I just chased it down. Arsenal's centre-half Jeff Blockley got murdered unfairly afterwards. He tried a back-pass to Bob Wilson in goal and I just latched onto it and knocked it in. The thing is, it bobbled as I hit it and it went in off my ankle bone. For a moment I thought I'd missed it."

JEFF BLOCKLEY

HALOM CELEBRATES THE OPENING GOAL

BOB WILSON

BILLY HUGHES

JIMMY HAMILTON

Sunderland squad member.

"It would have been nice to have been more involved with the squad. I was at the semi-final at Hillsborough. I was with all the youth and reserve lads and we were behind the goal on the terracing at the end where Vic Halom scored. That was a good Arsenal team but Bob Stokoe had Sunderland revved up and they were very aggressive. Dave Watson was a great player but Ritchie Pitt came to prominence at that time. This is where Micky Horswill came into it. As soon as the ball came to Micky, say 15 or 20 yards into his own half he would launch it into the corners. Hughesy, Dennis Tueart and Vic Halom knew he wasn't going to pull it down and pass it through. He was just going to launch it and that sent Arsenal back deep. They were good tactics. Sunderland didn't allow Arsenal to play and basically they did the same against Leeds.'

BOB WILSON

Arsenal goalkeeper.

"They never stopped running. They deserved to win."

BILLY HUGHES

Scorer of the winning goal.

" **To be honest it was not quite intended. It was a reflex action and I just got my head to a centre which Dennis Tueart flicked on. Luckily Bob Wilson was by the near post and all I can remember was the ball going into the net. How it got there I don't know because I was moving backwards.**"

*Billy Hughes passed away in 2019. This quote comes from an interview with Bernard Joy in the Evening Standard on the day of the cup final.

BOB STOKOE

The Messiah.

"People, grown men, were crying and bowing to me as though I was some kind of God that they were worshipping. It was then that I heard thousands of them calling me the messiah. I think that's when the press picked up on it. Tears rolled down my cheeks. Never in my life had I received such an ovation. I wanted to tell each and every one of them that this wasn't just my doing. It was a collective effort that included them. I walked off the pitch as I could feel myself breaking down with emotional joy."

*Bob Stokoe passed away in 2004. Quote taken from his biography 'Northern and Proud'

73

@FIFTY

THE FINAL

WE'VE WON
THE CUP

THE EMPIRE STADIUM, WEMBLEY

The Football Association
Challenge Cup
Competition

TURNSTILES
ENTRANCE

F

FINAL TIE

79

SAT., MAY 5, 1973

ROW

12

KICK-OFF 3 p.m.
YOU ARE ADVISED TO TAKE UP
YOUR POSITION BY 2.30 p.m.

SEAT

11

CHAIRMAN
WEMBLEY STADIUM LTD

No money refunded or tickets exchanged

NORTH STAND SEAT

£5.00

SEE PLAN AND CONDITIONS ON BACK

TO BE RETAINED

FOOTBALL ASSOCIATION CHALLENGE CUP COMPETITION

FINAL

LEEDS UNITED

V

SUNDERLAND

WEMBLEY STADIUM

JUBILEE 1923-1973

SATURDAY, 5th MAY, 1973 ... Kick

Official Programme . . . 15 pence

LONDON
EDITION

No. 31,601 (100th YEAR)

THEY'VE

This was the vital first goal which came after 31 minutes. The man who

Porterfield t
hero in glori
Wembley vic

— 1 LEEDS UNITED

SUNDERLAND

SUNDERLAND'S proudest
moment in 36 years arrived
at Wembley this afternoon
when they took on the might
of Leeds United, one of
British soccer's success sides
over the last ten years, in
the final of the F.A. Cup.
They carried with them the
own vociferous Wembley
a wealth of

73 @FIFTY

"Say Goodnight to Grandma" was the West End Show visited by members of the Leeds squad in the week leading up to the cup final, but at Wembley it was to be goodnight to their hopes of retaining the cup despite them being the most sizzling of red hot favourites.

Only four second division teams had ever won the FA Cup, the most recent being West Brom in 1931 when they were captained by former Sunderland West End player Tommy Glidden. In a season when they enjoyed a fine double by winning promotion, Albion had beaten struggling near neighbours Birmingham.

In 1912 West Brom were on the receiving end of an upset. The newly promoted Baggies were defeated in a replay by Barnsley who had finished sixth in Division Two while four years earlier there was a win for Wolves who had finished ninth in Division Two over Newcastle who had been fourth in the top-flight. The remaining win by a second division side was way back in 1894 when a hat-trick from former Sunderland forward James Logan helped Notts County to thrash Bolton Wanderers 4-1 in a season when Notts had been third top of their league while the Trotters had finished fourth bottom of Division One.

You had to look to 1949 for the last time a team ranked lower than Sunderland had reached the final - but on that occasion Leicester had lost 3-1 to Wolves. At the time of the 1973 final Sunderland were seventh. They would finish a place higher but there were no play-offs at this time.

Sunderland had been outside the second division relegation zone only on a marginally better goal average when Bob Stokoe took over in late November, under two weeks before the draw for the third round of the FA Cup was made. In contrast, opponents Leeds were the equivalent of facing Manchester City or Liverpool in 2023. Since being promoted with Sunderland in 1964 Leeds had never been out of the top four in Division One.

As well as being league champions in 1969, in the same period they had won two European trophies, the League Cup and were the FA Cup holders. The FA Cup final was not Leeds' only cup final of the month. Eleven days after United were due to meet Sunderland they had a date in Salonika in Greece where they were to play AC Milan in the final of the European Cup Winners' Cup. Watching them at Wembley would be Milan president Albino Buticchi as well as captain Gianni Rivera who had played at Roker Park for Italy in the 1966 World Cup.

Sunderland faced the most daunting of tasks. Despite their achievements in comprehensively disposing of two of the best teams in the land, few people outside of Wearside gave the Lads any chance. Even Manchester City's Malcolm Allison predicted a 3-0 win for Leeds. Given how the H-bombers had destroyed the City side Allison ran with Joe Mercer he might have known better.

Making their fourth appearance in the final in nine years, Leeds were considered by many to be nailed on to join a list of just four clubs to have ever retained a trophy first competed for over a century earlier.

Having had a flu epidemic shortly after Stokoe took over and then a long cup run that involved three replays Sunderland's preparations for Wembley were interrupted by a fixture pile-up.

On the Monday night before the trip to the old Twin Towers of the original Wembley Sunderland were in action in London, drawing 1-1 at Orient in front of under 10,000 with eight of the cup final team putting in a 90 minute shift. It was their tenth fixture in 31 days.

The squad set off for Selsdon Hall Golf and Country Club six days before the final, with that game at Orient to fulfil on the Monday. Several of the initial travelling party returned to Wearside to play in a cup final of their own. This was a reserve team cup final against Middlesbrough in which Maurice Hepworth was so badly injured by a kick in the stomach from Tony McAndrew that he could not even watch the FA Cup final on TV. Thankfully Hepworth fully recovered and was visited by the squad with the trophy as he fought back from a ruptured spleen, burst duodenum, ruptured bowel and ruptured intestines! Hepworth wasn't the only player with hospital worries, Ritchie Pitt's baby daughter was in hospital causing obvious worry to the key centre-back.

While a few fringe players had taken part in their own cup final the main men prepared for Wembley with serious training sessions combined with plenty of relaxation. The entire squad attended the Football Writers' Association Player of the Year dinner just two nights before the final while Dennis Tueart, Billy Hughes and Ian Porterfield had been to a recording of the BBC's flagship pop music programme 'Top of the Pops'. Hot Chocolate and Sweet would be amongst the groups they saw.

Sunderland never lost sight of the job they were there to do but they enjoyed a laugh too. There was no question of just enjoying the cup final and resigning themselves to being plucky losers against a ruthless top team. The players hadn't put in the graft to knock out Manchester City and Arsenal, not to mention the tricky quarter-final with Luton or the earlier rounds that had needed replays, just to come this far and meekly accept defeat. That was evident from Ritchie Pitt's robust first-minute challenge on Allan Clarke.

In contrast, regardless of their night out at the theatre, the vastly experienced Leeds were the team who looked as if they might have a dose of stage fright. In the days of wall to wall TV coverage of the cup final on both main channels from early in the morning, infamously Leeds in their club suits looked stiff and nervous in their pre-match interview from their team hotel.

On the other hand, Sunderland's players looked as if they didn't have a care in the world when the cameras rolled at Selsdon Hall, collapsing in hysterics as Billy Hughes produced a laughing box which he set off whenever anyone was asked a question. Sunderland were saving the serious business for later.

Attendances having hit rock bottom before Stokoe's arrival, Sunderland had taken off so sensationally that the clamour for tickets massively outstripped supply. Regardless of the fact that so many of the tickets earmarked for neutrals by the FA ended up in the hands of Sunderland supporters there were never going to be anywhere near enough to satisfy demand. Even future long-serving chairman and lifetime supporter Bob Murray was unable to procure one.

TRAINING AT SELSDON HALL

75

SUNDERLAND

WEMBLEY '73

GPO

the official brochure of SUNDERLAND

PRICE
30p

GREETINGS TELEGRAM ✳

V 9/5

E58 AP8 1.1 PM NEWCASTLEONTYNE T

ALLPURPOSE

THE MAYOR OF SUNDERLAND CIVIC CENTRE SUNDERLAND =

NEWCASTLE WISHES SUNDERLAND THE BEST OF LUCK

AT WEMBLEY TOMORROW STOP THE ENGLISH CUP AT

ROKER WOULD BE A GOOD OMEN FOR THE

NEW TYNE AND WEAR AUTHORITY =

ARTHUR GREY LORD MAYOR NEWCASTLEONTYNE +

"I couldn't get a ticket for the match" became a mantra of so many desperate fans. Someone who did have a ticket was Billy Butterfield of the Sunderland Echo. The main SAFC writer, operating under the name of Argus, in the 'Football' Echo, the week before the final he wrote with pride, "…in the vast crowd which will gather for the show game of the season there will be no one more thrilled than myself. For nearly 25 years I have been rejecting my right to attend the Cup Final every year, waiting patiently for the day when Sunderland would win their way there. There has been a lot of laughter over the years from those who saw humour in my optimism. But it has been worth waiting for and in seven days' time I will be going to my first Cup final with a Sunderland team bursting with pride and determination to make it a day to remember."

Someone else who must have been bursting with pride was Bob Stokoe who had transformed the town and the team. Ten days before the final, following a board meeting it was announced that Stokoe had signed a five-year contract.

Stokoe and Leeds manager Don Revie had been direct opponents in the 1955 FA Cup final when Stokoe as Newcastle's centre-half came out on top against Revie who was Manchester City's centre-forward under the management of former Sunderland player Les McDowall. There was absolutely no love lost between Stokoe and Revie, nor was there any love lost between Sunderland and Leeds, as outlined in the earlier 'Meanwhile back in Sunderland' chapter.

Stokoe had accused Revie of attempted bribery and match fixing when Stokoe was manager of Bury, accusing Revie of offering him £500 to throw one of the two late-season matches Bury had with Leeds in the early sixties (See page 74 of Stokoe's biography, 'Northern and Proud' by Paul Harrison).

Such allegations against Revie were not unheard of in this era. They had re-surfaced in the season of the cup final with Sunderland when the Sunday People alleged that attempts had been made to fix Leeds' league title decider against Wolves the previous May. Three Wanderers players: David Wagstaffe, Frank Munro and Bernard Shaw were reported to have accused telephone callers of trying to bribe them. There appeared to be no evidence that these calls came from Leeds officials and Revie refused to countenance them, stating, "I have never heard anything so ridiculous in my life."

Prioritising the cup final against one of his old clubs Sunderland, Revie rotated his side for league games leading up to Wembley with a host of squad players (including future Sunderland man Frank Gray) being used. There was also a scare for Trevor Cherry. He apparently suffered from concussion sustained in a game with Southampton. As a consequence it was reported that a potential suspension was delayed when his appeal against a caution had to be postponed.

Cherry would play at Wembley and be one of the two players thwarted by Monty's famous double-save. As ever under Revie, Leeds' preparation was meticulous but nothing could have prepared them for the red and white tidal wave they were about to face.

THE GAME

Monty's double-save, Ian Porterfield's goal and Ritchie Pitt's tackle are the three incidents that most people pick out as iconic moments from the actual game with Stokoe's final-whistle run to Monty added to the mental showreel. Overriding these key moments is the over-arching understanding that it was togetherness and teamwork throughout the side that provided the basis for the moments that won the cup.

As thousands travelled from the north east by road, rail and air there was morning rain to welcome people to the capital. Before the match there was a full programme of events to keep supporters entertained but of course it was the football everyone was there for. Instead of pre-match community singing the FA introduced top class athletics which included top UK 3,000m runner David Bedford who was beaten by Belgian world record holder and Olympic silver medallist Emiel Puttemains. Dave Herron of Lincolnshire beat an all GB field in an 800m event. The athletics followed a programme of music by the combined bands of the Scots and Welsh Guards and preceded a display by the Ayr Majorettes before star singer Frankie Vaughan led the singing of the traditional and stirring cup final hymn 'Abide with Me'.

Finally, the teams were presented to the President of the FA, HRH The Duke of Kent and at last the players could break away from the ceremonial preliminaries, begin to warm up and ditch their personalised tracksuit tops.

As the referee called the two Scottish captains together Leeds' Billy Bremner at 5' 5" towered over Sunderland's 5' 4" Bobby Kerr. Referee Ken Burns had history with Leeds. After they had controversially beaten Sunderland after two replays in the FA Cup fifth round in 1967, Leeds knocked out Manchester City and met Chelsea in the semi-final where they lost after having two apparently legitimate goals disallowed by Burns. He had been a linesman in the FA Cup final of 1969 and by 1973 was president of the Referees' Association.

There had been no dilemma about Stokoe's selection. No-one went to Wembley wondering what the line-up would be, unless there was to be a late and unexpected injury. The only question would be who would get the nod to be the single substitute allowed in those days. In the end Brian Chambers who was listed in the match programme was replaced by David Young who had scored in the previous Monday's 1-1 draw at Orient.

Both teams were settled sides. Eight players in each line-up had played in every game of their respective cup runs. In Leeds' case two others had missed just a single match. No-one on either side had scored as many FA Cup goals that season as England striker Allan 'Sniffer' Clarke. He had scored the winner in the previous year's final and had netted six this time around. If he was dreaming of another he was brought down to earth with a thud after less than a minute when Ritchie Pitt wiped him out with a tackle that spelled out to all concerned that Sunderland might be in Division Two but they meant business.

73

IAN PORTERFIELD

"The time was 3.31 and 31 seconds precisely. The date: Saturday May 5 this year. The moment when time stood still for me. Never in all my life have I felt such emotion.It swelled up in my throat until it almost choked me. Sunderland, my club, were ahead in the FA Cup final at Wembley and I had scored the all-important goal."

*Ian Porterfield passed away in 2007. Quote taken from Ian's book, "The Impossible Dream" written with John Gibson 1973.

Given Leeds' reputation for rough play they could hardly grumble. If Messrs Hunter, Bremner, Giles and co wanted to dish it out they would find that there were no shrinking violets in red and white. Ritchie would probably see red for that 'tackle' nowadays but this wasn't nowadays, it was 1973 when such challenges were normal. To his chagrin Clarke would be the first man booked, for a tackle on Hughes 20 minutes later.

Having won the toss Sunderland got on the front foot by starting the game attacking the end where most of their vociferous supporters were based. First to touch the ball for the red and whites was Tueart. In typical style Dennis drove straight at the heart of the opponents defence. When his shot was blocked two of his teammates slipped to the ground as they tried to put the brakes on, such was the surface after the pre-match rain which had briefly relented but started to drizzle again during the presentation to the royal guest.

Immediately the pace was fast and furious. Both teams wanted to get straight onto the front foot. Leeds seemed set on putting the second division upstarts in their place while Sunderland were going for the jugular, as they had done with Arsenal. Whereas in modern football many teams try to pass each other to death, keeping possession and probing for the perfect opening, there was nothing unusual in the seventies about both teams attacking directly: you attack, we attack.

Eleven of the twelve named by Leeds were full internationals. The odd man out was Trevor Cherry who was in his first season with the club. He went on to captain England. Of the Sunderland side no-one was yet a full international (Watson, Tueart and Hughes would go on to be) and only Pitt had played at Wembley before, in a schoolboy international. However such was the belief in the Roker ranks that there was absolutely no inkling of an inferiority complex. More to the point there was no need to have one. Sunderland's Team of 73 were a brilliant side whose time had come.

The opening half hour saw both teams fight for a first goal. For Leeds, Lorimer, Gray and Hunter shot wide while Giles and Clarke had shots blocked, Watson doing brilliantly to thwart Clarke. At the other end Sunderland played in several threatening balls that just eluded their forwards with a Hughes effort from a Porterfield pass being the Wearsiders' best effort, only for it to go over the top.

Another attempt that looked like going over the top was a looping cross shot by captain Kerr, but this dipped to threaten keeper Harvey. Faced with a wet slippery ball Harvey chose to help it on its way over the bar rather than trying to catch a ball that could have been like trying to hold a bar of soap, especially as Hughes was rushing in to pounce if there was the slightest slip.

The magical goal that won the cup came from the corner, just as corners had produced both goals in the quarter-final. Hughes took it and aimed for the towering Watson. So concerned were Leeds about Dave that they double marked him but the ball went beyond the future England centre-half to Halom. He took a touch and knocked it into his own path.

Vic might have got a close range shot in but the ball came to
Porterfield who controlled it on his left thigh before smashing
it into the net from eight yards with his right foot. By his own
admission Ian normally only used his right foot for standing on.
So much so that as the scorer of the winning goal in the cup final
he received a prize of the time of a golden boot and despite scoring
with his right foot asked for the golden boot to be a left one.

73

@FIFTY

"And Sunderland have done what they threatened to do" boomed the BBC commentator David Coleman. From my seat in line with the edge of the 18-yard box I can remember the rain that had settled on the net cascading down in shimmering light as Porterfield's shot struck the back of the net. As those droplets left the netting it was like a weight being lifted.

Going into the game there had been a belief in the players and supporters that the rest of the country could stuff the idea of Sunderland being giant-killers. Sunderland had always been true giants of the game themselves and now they were playing like it. This was happening in front of our eyes, not being read in the history books. The first goal in any game is important and Sunderland had got it. "We shall not be moved" sang the crowd and Jimmy Montgomery as much as anyone else saw to that.

The 'Football' Echo headlines 'They've Done it!' and 'Porterfield the hero in glorious Wembley victory' are rightly well known but the back page of that same Sports Echo report was aptly headlined, "Second half saw 'Monty' in top form." This is not to say Leeds were massively on top but even if they got past a committed defence marshalled by the magnificent Watson there was still to be no way past 'The Mighty Jim.'

Just as Arsenal hard-man Peter Storey had been cautioned shortly after Sunderland had opened the scoring in the semi-final, Leeds' Billy Bremner didn't take kindly to going behind. Within a minute or two of the goal he launched a scything tackle from behind on Horswill but escaped any more punishment than a lecture from the referee. Given Pitt hadn't been booked for his early tackle on Clarke the referee was at least being consistent.

Horswill was an unsung hero of the cup run. The youngest member of the team at 20, he superbly nullified superstars Colin Bell and Alan Ball of Manchester City and Arsenal and in the final largely divided his attention between the twin turbo of the Leeds midfield, Bremner and Giles. Horswill found the energy in the final to pepper Leeds goal with several efforts of his own but was also on the receiving end of more than one naughty challenge, needing treatment after one particular foul by Giles.

Half-time came with Sunderland in the ascendancy but Leeds were obviously still a big danger given their pedigree. Stokoe's Stars had been the better team and deserved the lead but with an old head like Stokoe in charge the players were completely aware of the fact that the job was only half done. The crowd didn't need any whipping up but as the team emerged from the tunnel behind the far end to where the main Sunderland support was, as Bobby Kerr approached the end he'd be defending in the second half he whirled his arms like windmills to urge yet more spirit and noise from the massed ranks of red and whites.

73 @FIFTY

DICK MALONE

Defender who cleared the ball after Monty's famous double-save.

"If you've got the cup final on DVD watch it, and just before Jimmy's save you'll see
me stumble. You watch why I'm stumbling - Allan Clarke had actually tripped me because
when the ball was coming across to Trevor Cherry I could have headed it clear, but he
tripped me, otherwise I'd have cleared it, but Trevor Cherry headed it goalwards and
Peter Lorimer had a dig. I felt if that had gone in I would have chinned the referee."

JIM MONTGOMERY

On 'THE' save.

"I can see it in my mind as it happened. I can picture the ball coming
in from the right from Paul Reaney. I see Dick [Malone] stumble
and Cherry coming in on the far post to make the initial
header. The rest was just reaction. I can vividly see the
ball going to a white shirt so therefore it was a case
of just getting up as quickly as possible"...

The second half began as the first did with Sunderland threatening initially before Leeds came forward. Determined to get back onto level terms as soon as possible Leeds actually had the ball in the net shortly after the re-start but the 'goal' was disallowed. Just as he would do later in the game when he fouled Dick Malone off the ball a split second before Monty's miraculous double save, Alan Clarke fouled Montgomery before Trevor Cherry knocked the ball into the goal. Referee Burns was quick to spot the offence and gave Sunderland a free-kick.

Sunderland went close themselves when it took some determined defending by the Yorkshire side as Hughes and Porterfield had shots beaten out before Ron Guthrie fired in an effort which flew into the side netting. Soon afterwards Guthrie powered in another shot from distance that went narrowly wide and looking to add to his quarter-final goal the left-back fired in yet another shot a few minutes later as Sunderland looked to double their lead.

At no point in the final was it one-way traffic in either direction and so Leeds came again. Not long after Lorimer had shot into the side-netting came one of the most iconic moments of any final. Sixty-six minutes had gone when Reaney floated in a ball from the right. Aiming for his full-back partner Cherry on the far post the ball might have been cut out by Malone. Shortly before Porterfield's goal Malone's height at the back stick had been invaluable as he won an important header with white shirts queueing up behind him ready to pounce.

On this occasion as Dick tried to deal with the delivery, Clarke cutely clipped his heels to knock him off balance and leave Cherry free to strike. As ever, Montgomery was there but all he could do was parry the ball into the danger area. As in the film 'Jaws' which came out a couple of years later, the feeling of relief at having escaped disaster was replaced within a split-second by a feeling of terror as a bigger threat emerged. The great white shirt of Peter Lorimer loomed large over the loose ball. The man renowned to have the hardest shot in football had the goal - and Sunderland's fate - at his mercy. Had he scored Leeds would have had the momentum, not to mention the experience, to go on and wrap up the win and leave the Lads as gallant losers.

Would that have happened or would the red and whites have shown the resilience they did in the fifth round replay to fight off Manchester City when Franny Lee halved Stokoe's men's lead? We will never know, but we don't have to because despite TV commentator Coleman proclaiming, "And Lorimer makes it one each" it wasn't 1-1 because Monty had magnificently produced the greatest save Wembley has ever seen.

Monty was a fantastic goalkeeper with reflexes second to none. In his career he made better saves than this one but this was in the cup final being beamed around the world when hardly any football outside the World Cup finals and European Cup final was seen globally.

The watching world and the TV commentators were stunned and surprised but the Sunderland supporters behind the goal weren't.

They had been used to Monty's magic for a decade and responded with a heartfelt chant of, 'Jimmy, Jimmy Monty, lalalalalalala'. A moment after declaring Leeds had equalised Coleman corrected himself, "No! Astonishing! They're appealing to the referee. Lorimer thought he'd scored. Most of the crowd did but it wasn't in."

Even when he was afforded a replay a couple of minutes later the commentator evidently couldn't imagine just how good a save it had been, "It came off the goalkeeper" he said but the Sunderland fans knew it was one of Monty's miracle saves and soon so did the rest of the world.

It was the moment that made Montgomery world famous and it rightly reinforced Jim's stature as a truly legendary figure in the entire history of the football club. What's more it made Leeds realise that no matter how good they were and no matter what they did they weren't going to score. Sunderland's name was on the cup.

Many, including me, thought it had been since the fifth round tie at Manchester City when the sleeping giant was roused. Revie had witnessed the replay with City, so deep down in his bones on the Leeds bench he would have known Sunderland were capable of anything, no matter how good his team were.

Lorimer was a great player who frightened the living daylights out of many an opponent - but not Monty. In the run up to the final Jim had been asked about the Scotland international whose shots had been measured at up to 90 miles per hour. "I have faced harder shots than Peter's" Jim had admitted, "The hardest shot that I have come across was packed by Walsall's Colin Taylor. Colin had a dynamic shot in either foot and it was always a little worrying when he was around the penalty area." Known as Cannonball Colin, Taylor had scored the first two goals Montgomery ever conceded in 1961.

Fifty years on people are still talking about Monty's double save, especially the second stop. It seemed to knock the stuffing out of the men from Elland Road. With quarter of an hour left they withdrew Eddie Gray who many so-called experts had predicted would be the match-winner. Coming back from injury Gray never got a look in against Malone and Kerr whose game plan to mark him out of the match worked perfectly. Revie realised 'Super-Dick's capabilities. He had tried to sign him before Malone left Ayr United for Sunderland.

Substitute Terry Yorath tested Montgomery soon after coming on but once again he might as well have not bothered. Monty was the biggest barrier the north of England had seen since the Roman Wall and he wasn't going to be beaten. If there was to be another goal in the closing stages it was going to be at the other end as Sunderland looked to make it 2-0.

David Harvey made a superb flying save to fingertip away a drive from Halom who took the chance to put both Harvey and the ball into the back of the net the next time he got an opportunity. It was the last incident of a wonderful match as moments later the referee blew for time. The cup would have red and white ribbons.

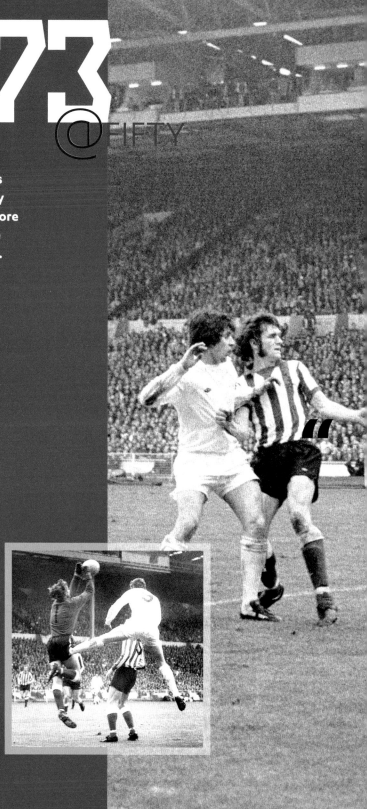

73 @FIFTY

BOB STOKOE
On Monty's save.

"My heart sank when I saw the ball falling to Lorimer, he just didn't miss from that range. I turned my head toward the Leeds bench in anticipation of seeing them leap in the air. They very nearly did, but then a look of absolute horror and despair came across their faces."

*Bob Stokoe passed away in 2004. Quote taken from his biography 'Northern and Proud'.

JIM MONTGOMERY
On 'THE' save.

"I spoke to Peter Lorimer many times since and he said he couldn't have hit it more sweetly than he did but that was the only vacant space. I saw him hit the ball and I saw the ball clearly. It was a case of getting something there and diverting it. Fortunately it hit the bar and came back down but yes I remember it vividly. Dick got the ball away for a throw in so you couldn't think of anything but dealing with the next situation of the throw in."

JIM MONTGOMERY

On Bob Stokoe running to him at the final whistle.

"First of all when the whistle went I just turned around to the supporters and had my hands in the air. The next thing was I turned around and Bob was nearly on top of me. I didn't see him come from the start, so the next thing I knew he was jumping up - well we tried to jump up but we weren't quite in sync. Either he was jumping and I was coming down or vice-versa.

Ron Guthrie came over, Bobby came and took his cap and a supporter came on. I remember that vividly but what Bob said I have no idea because of the crescendo of the noise of the crowd and everything that was going on. It wasn't until weeks later when Bob and I met up for lunch or a cup of coffee or whatever that I asked him the question. He just said it was because of the saves I'd made throughout the cup run, particularly those from Les Bradd at Notts County and George Armstrong in the semi-final as well as the double-save in the final."

73 @FIFTY

As those ribbons were being attached Stokoe sprinted to Montgomery. All tracksuit and trilby, mac flowing behind him as the former centre-half showed pace more akin to a winger. Stokoe was only 42 at the time and had indelibly imprinted his name into Wearside folklore - as had all the FA Cup winners who truly were Stokoe's Stars.

As Bobby Kerr lifted the trophy and Sunderland took their lap of honour the joy of the cup winners was obvious as was normal, but this was not normal, as BBC radio commentator Peter Jones said, "You have never seen scenes like this at a cup final before." He was right and what is more such scenes have never been seen again and nor are they ever likely to be.

No team had been league champions more than Sunderland at the time of World War Two. Sunderland were the only club to have only ever played in the top-flight at the time Stokoe was a cup winner as a player in 1955, but since then and the financial scandal that followed in the late fifties Sunderland had plumbed the lowest ebbs in their entire history. Six months before this glorious day at Wembley Sunderland had been staring at an unprecedented drop into the third tier. Bob Stokoe, the son of a coal-mining life-time Sunderland supporter had come back to his native north east and electrified Wearside. As Bob said, and as it says on the plinth of his statue, "I didn't bring the magic. It's always been there. I just came back to find it."

SUNDERLAND: Montgomery, Malone, Guthrie, Horswill, Watson, Pitt, Kerr, Hughes, Halom, Porterfield, Tueart. Sub: Young.

LEEDS UNITED: Harvey, Reaney, Cherry, Bremner, Madeley, Hunter, Lorimer, Clarke, Jones, Giles, Gray (Yorath 75).

REFEREE: Mr K Burns (Stourbridge).

MICK HORSWILL

On Billy Hughes' laughing box.

"In those days David Coleman and the TV, or whoever it was, used to go to the different camps in the hotels. You lined up with the big lads at the back and everyone else on seats at the front. They interviewed a couple of the Leeds lads at their hotel and then they came to us. I can't remember who was asked the first question. None of us knew Billy Hughes had turned up with a laughing box in his pocket so the questions never got answered because every time someone got asked a question he set it off and we couldn't stop laughing. It was hilarious but that's the way we were, we were dead relaxed on the day.

"I was just a young lad and only ever got nervous once. I just wanted to get on the pitch and get on with it. The only time I got nervous was at the final and that was because in those days when you came out you lined up facing each other, not in one line like they do now. When they played the national anthem you had to stand facing your opponents, so I was looking at Allan Clarke all the time but as soon as it was finished I could get it back into my head that we were going to get into them straight away."

DENNIS TUEART

Also on the laughing box.

"Without question, Billy's laughing box illustrated that we weren't at all phased by the occasion. We were very relaxed during our television interview whereas Leeds were all very regimental in their club suits. We didn't have to wear club suits. We were told we could wear what we liked for the final. We had the free expression to be ourselves and that free expression was reflected in the way Billy brought out the laughing box and in the way we played."

JOE ANDERSON

Sunderland supporter then based in Essex.

"My mum and my sister were in with the Sunderland end but I was in the Leeds end near the tunnel with my dad. I didn't have to worry about being quiet so as not to give myself away because there were loads of Sunderland supporters in the Leeds end."

JOE BOLTON

Had played in the first two games of the cup run.

"I can remember I had Dick Malone's Crombie on and I had Billy Hughes' teeth in one pocket and Bobby Kerr's in the other. I thought, 'Will I give them the wrong ones?' I thought they might go up to get the Cup with the wrong teeth in, and I was worried in case I gave them the wrong ones by accident."

73

@FIFTY

F.A. CUP FINAL
1973

93

VIC HALOM

Sunderland's Wembley centre-forward.

"The owners of the hotel had a Rolls Royce and I hired it for my parents. It picked them up in the morning, took them for lunch and I'd ordered some champagne so it was a very special day for them. My mum said she felt like the Queen of England driving down Wembley Way with a great big red and white rosette on the Rolls."

MICK HORSWILL

The youngest member of the cup-winning team.

"There were only two things about the day that spoilt it for me. One was the Queen wasn't there because I was dying to meet the Queen but she wasn't there to present the cup. The other thing was Ritchie's first-minute tackle on Allan Clarke. I didn't like it because I wish it had been me!

"Modern supporters might not realise how good Leeds were but it was like playing Manchester City or Liverpool now, but we never even mentioned them. I can't remember ever sitting down and thinking, 'Wow, we're playing against Bremner and Hunter and Giles and so on. It was the same right the way through including when we played against Manchester City and Arsenal. All we wanted to do was get out there and get at them because we knew we were a good side. Nobody mentioned the other team at all."

DICK MALONE

On Sunderland's support.

"**I remember when we left the Selsdon Park Golf & Country Club at Croydon, all we saw between there and Wembley was people wearing red and white scarves. When we came out onto the pitch three-quarters of the stadium was red and white. It was unbelieveable."**

DANNY BLANCHFLOWER

Twice an FA Cup winning captain with Tottenham Hotspur, writing in the Sunday Express.

"Raise your glasses to the greatest tonic English football has had for years. The toast is Sunderland - the finest team of heroes to carry off the FA Cup in my experience of Wembley. It was the most gripping, emotional final I have been to and that included the two in which I carried off that cup. The Sunderland crowd were marvellous.

They brought a breath of fresh air to Wembley from the North East, full of warmth and humour and love for the game as well as their team. Their team were magnificent. When I saw these players earlier in the season I never thought they could play like this. They were great ...Sunderland you were wonderful for football."

DON REVIE

Leeds manager and former Sunderland player.

"We have no excuses. This is how cup finals go. I do not want to take anything away from Sunderland. Full credit to them. They all played well."

*Don Revie died in 1989. Quote taken from Don Warters, Soccer writer for the Yorkshire Evening Post in a Sunderland produced magazine called "We've done it."

DICK MALONE

On nullifying Leeds dangerman Eddie Gray.

"Bobby [Kerr] and I always worked as a unit. Bob [Stokoe] didn't need to say anything to us about specifically dealing with Eddie Gray. I never felt anything about it at all. Apparently the pundits felt because of the marauding runs I was known for Leeds would be able to get Gray in behind me and that he'd expose me, which was fair comment. What they failed to understand is I knew that's what they thought, so I wouldn't do the marauding runs up the park and give them the space to do that.

"Jack Charlton had said on the television that he thought Eddie Gray would exploit the space I'd leave behind me when I went forward. When you're on a panel on TV and you are asked for an opinion you've got to come up with something. I did attack a lot but Bobby Kerr and I decided that in the final I wouldn't attack a lot and we'd smother him in the space that I was supposed to leave and that's what happened.

"If I did go forward then Bobby defended and took charge but I stayed back most of the time. No disrespect to Eddie Gray because he was a brilliant player and he had just come back from injury but to be honest when he was substituted, at the time I didn't know he'd been taken off. That is the God's honest truth. When I was playing I just thought about my actions."

EDDIE GRAY

Leeds and Scotland winger.

"There's no doubt that these days the players from both sides of the 1973 cup final have a mutual respect for each other. There was no hard feelings on our part after the game when it was all finished. Obviously we were disappointed to lose the cup final but on the day Sunderland did the job that they had to do. They all stuck to their task and they ended up winning the FA Cup.

"Jim Montgomery had a terrific game that day but so did the rest of the players. Dick Malone, Dave Watson, Ritchie Pitt and Ron Guthrie were all strong and when you look at the midfield area of Bobby Kerr and Micky Horswill it was a strong midfield with Ian Porterfield scoring the goal.

With Billy Hughes, Vic Halom and Dennis Tueart up front it was a strong side. There were a lot of good players in that team, especially when you consider what the likes of Dennis Tueart and Dave Watson went on to achieve in their careers. Billy Hughes was a fantastic player whose brother [John] I used to watch playing for Celtic.

"It's all credit to Sunderland. When you actually analyse the FA Cup that year Sunderland had beaten Manchester City and Arsenal as well. I think it was written in the Gods that they were going to win the Cup. I don't think there's any doubt about it that in the final we were the better team but Sunderland played well and did the job they had to do. Jim Montgomery's save from Peter Lorimer was just out of this world.

"The way Sunderland played wasn't a surprise to us. Don [Revie] had emphasised to us how tough it was going to be plus the fact there was the attitude of their manager - he didn't like losing! We knew it was going to be a battle and all credit to them for sticking it out. It was great for Sunderland Football Club. That's the great thing about football. Everybody in the country was probably thinking we would win the game by three or four but we never thought like that. We knew it was going to be tough because we knew what they had already done in the FA Cup that year. We were flying high and we were the team to beat and won the league the next year.

"I used to love playing at Roker Park because there was a great atmosphere there with the fans being so passionate but the cup final was a huge disappointment for me personally and for us as a club. I had been playing well at that time but I had a terrible game in the Cup final and that's all credit to Dick Malone and his teammates. You've got to give them credit for that but my good friend Bob Murray never lets me forget it!"

DANNY BLANCHFLOWER

Former Northern Ireland captain on Malone's mastery of Gray.

"What a great game Malone had. He stuffed Eddie Gray down the throats of those Leeds players and officials who claimed that Gray would be the matchwinner. In the second half Revie subbed Yorath for Gray and that was Malone's tribute."

JOHN BYRNE

1992 FA Cup semi-final goalscorer.

"I remember that final as a kid. I'd be twelve and was living in Manchester. Jimmy Montgomery's save was absolutely brilliant. What a great occasion and Sunderland deserved it."

DAVID YOUNG

Sunderland's only substitute.

"All the time I kept thinking I might be brought on. Two or three times Stokoe told me to get warmed up so I ran up and down the side of the pitch for a few minutes and they forgot about me so I sat back down again but eventually I realised I wasn't getting on. I didn't know I'd be substitute until the morning of the game.

On the Monday before Wembley I played and scored in the 1-1 draw at Orient. I was thrilled to get the chance to play in that game. I really worked hard and played well. That and the fact I could play in a few positions helped me to get the nod for the number twelve shirt.

"I'd damaged my knee in a league game at Sheffield Wednesday. I had to come off in the first few minutes. Ritchie Pitt was on loan and came straight back and that was it, Ritchie was back in the team and I couldn't get back in again. It's always been lovely to be part of the 1973 cup final squad. It's been amazing and I've really enjoyed it and I always like to bring my medal to functions to show people."

RON GUTHRIE

**Wembley left-back who went close
to scoring on several occasions.**

"In the cup final Bob Stokoe offered all the defenders
33/1 to not let a goal in, saying if we gave him a
pound he'd give us each £33 if we kept a clean sheet
and I think the forwards got the same if they scored.
He paid up as well!"

73

@FIFTY

LINDA HUGHES

Widow of Billy Hughes.

"**Billy stayed up all night singing 'Ee-aye-adio, we won the cup' through the corridors of the hotel, to the point it drove everybody mad when everyone was desperate for sleep and Billy wasn't having any of it. He stayed up with Brian Connolly who was the lead singer of the pop group The Sweet. Suzy Quattro and Hot Chocolate were also on that night at the Grosvenor Hotel. They were all performing at the official banquet.**

"I spent most of the night talking to Brian Connolly's wife and then the following day the wives brought the cup up to Sunderland as the team went off to play a game at Cardiff on the Monday night. I've still got my ticket and rosette from the match itself. I was in seat 13 as I recall and I think I spent most of the match under the seat with nerves! I don't think I saw much of the game!"

MICKY HORSWILL

Cup final hero.

"I remember The Sweet, Suzy Quattro and Hot Chocolate being on and there was also Alan Price who was a Sunderland supporter. He was playing on the piano while some of us were stood on it because we were a bit tipsy by then! The thing was we were walking around all night talking to everybody so the lads never ate anything. It got to about one or two in the morning and me, Ian, Ritchie, Dennis and Billy left the hotel on Park Lane to go and find something to eat. After we walked for a while the first place we came to was a burger bar which was choc-a-bloc with Sunderland supporters when half of the team walked in. It was chaos!"

DENNIS TUEART

Wembley winner.

"Me, Micky and Billy had been down to Rak Records at their studios at Curzon Street in London with Mickie Most who was a well-known producer at the time. They produced our cup final record we recorded with the comedian Bobby Knoxall. Rak Records had just signed Suzi Quattro so they were keen to promote her at our banquet. The week before the cup final Billy, Micky and me had been on the Emperor Rosko lunchtime show.

"Because of our time with Alan Brown before Bob Stokoe came in, what we had in the background was a disciplined approach to our own performance. A lot of us were young kids who had come through the youth team at Sunderland and we had a combination of a disciplined mentality inbuilt in us by Alan Brown, along with the freedom of expression given to us by Bob Stokoe. From a Leeds point of view it was a lethal combination. Most of us had grown up together in the same team. Bob made training a bit more light-hearted. It was intense but we also enjoyed ourselves. It was the second half of the season so we had a lot of games so we didn't need a massive training programme. We didn't get any injuries so we had a settled side.

"We didn't have any fear, we just had excitement because we had never been to Wembley before. We didn't know what to expect. It was all brand new to us. We were like a bunch of lads going into an exciting party atmosphere. All of the supporters were having one long party and were having a whale of a time."

JIMMY HAMILTON

Sunderland squad member, but one of those to miss out on the cup run.

"We played to our strengths. In the final the game fizzed by but what I do remember is that I got two tickets that we could give to family. I sent mine up to my dad in Glasgow. He came down by train with a mate of his so you had two rough and tumble lads from Glasgow. I'd said to my dad, 'I'll meet you between the twin towers' at about half past two - quarter to three. I didn't realise the gap between the twin towers and there were thousands of people milling about so I didn't see my dad plus I think he was the worse for wear having come down on the sleeper. I phoned him up the day after and he'd had a carry out with the Sunderland fans on the way home."

MALCOLM BRAMLEY

Former assistant secretary at Sunderland.

"The thing that sticks in the memory is Ritchie Pitt's tackle on Allan Clarke in the first minute. I think everyone agrees that if that had been now he'd have been sent off straight away but it wasn't unusual in that era. That tackle set our stall out that showed we meant business and made Leeds realise they had a game on their hands. The way Sunderland won the cup was unique and the players who were involved have become part of the folklore of the club. In the years to come the Sunderland players will become more and more immortalised in history."

BOBBY KERR

Sunderland captain, 'The Little General'.

I'm very proud to have been Sunderland's captain in the cup final. It's still the case that no matter where I go people recognise me as being one of the cup final players and it's brilliant to have that.

"The thing I remember most about being presented with the cup is that on the way down to the pitch I slipped when I turned the corner to come off the wood and onto the concrete. In the game itself the goal came from a corner after I put the ball into the middle. People sometimes ask me if that was meant to be a shot or a cross. I had just tried to cross it into the box. I tried to keep it away from the goalkeeper but it dropped right under the bar and he just tipped it over the top for a corner as he didn't want to risk trying to catch it as Billy Hughes was running in."

73 **@FIFTY**

THE HOMECOMING
STOKOE'S
STARS

FOOTBALL
EDITION
TONIGHT

No. 31,604 (100th YEAR)

WELL DONE SUNDERLAND

PICTURES OF
WELCOME HOME
TOMORROW

Echo
SUNDERLAND

TUESDAY, MAY 8,

No. 31,603 (100th YEAR)

WELCOME HOM

Council move to confer rare honour on team

SUNDERLAND Town Council is to be asked to confer the Freedom of the Borough on Sunderland A.F.C. manager, Mr Bob Stokoe, and his Cup-winning team.

Coun. Charles Slater, Leader of the Council's Labour Group said he will ask the Council to grant the honorary Freedom of the Borough to Mr Stokoe for his achievements since taking over as Sunderland manager.

He said he was also considering putting the Cup-winning team forward for the same honour and the move is expected to be approved following the historic victory

Play-it-cool plea
at tonight's

"WELCOME back, stars" say the reg the Board Inn, E rington. They wi in force tonight banner as th ride into the Sunderland t coach with t

With them to goal-scoring Steven Porterfiel up the Drive. Steven (3) specia

Wearside is re
to show its he
once agai

What the
Echo says

IT'S all going to before and happen again night
EY came not in th ndreds or thousands, but s of thousands. They essed themselves and their omes overall in red a hite

73

@FIFTY

WEDNESDAY, MAY 9, 1973   3p

cho
DERLAND

• OPEN SIX DAYS UNTIL 6.0 P.M.

Binns
3 DAY MENSWEAR

Having won the cup on the Saturday it might be imagined that the team brought the cup home the day after for the traditional open topped bus tour. That would have been great but the fixture pile up that had seen Sunderland fulfil a league fixture on the Monday night before Wembley meant that they had another game to play on the Monday after Wembley - at Cardiff. The trophy would be paraded on the Tuesday before the final league fixture on the Wednesday, against already promoted Queen's Park Rangers.

Seven years later West Ham would come to Roker Park on the Monday after they won the cup for a vital match for Sunderland where a point was needed to secure promotion. (Sunderland won 2-0). When it was the Lads' turn to play just two days after running around Wembley with the cup the venue was Ninian Park, Cardiff. The Bluebirds required a point to stay up. They did have the safety net of another opportunity as other than the Sunderland v QPR game the only other outstanding fixture in the division was another home game for Cardiff with Hull on the same night Sunderland were due to entertain QPR. If the Welsh side collected a point they would survive and Huddersfield Town would fall through the relegation trapdoor.

Cardiff were managed by Jimmy Scoular, Stokoe's skipper when he won the cup as a player with Newcastle in 1955. Replaced by Joe Bolton, Ron Guthrie was the only member of the cup final side not to play in a game where the home side took what for them was a vital lead seven minutes before half-time through Bobby Woodruff.

Somehow dredging up the energy Sunderland equalised seven minutes after the re-start through Vic Halom in front of Cardiff's biggest gate of the season, 26,008. The game finished 1-1, Scoular's side taking the point they craved. Mathematically they could have still gone down had Hull beaten them by the unimaginable margin of 11-0 48 hours later but a 2-0 win for the Tigers was sufficient to relegate their Yorkshire rivals and keep Cardiff up.

As Sunderland played at Cardiff 48 hours after the final Leeds took on Celtic in a testimonial for Jack Charlton who had just been installed as manager of Middlesbrough.

On the Wednesday as SAFC entertained QPR Leeds thrashed Arsenal 6-1 in the league with a Lorimer hat-trick. However they would go on to lose the European Cup Winners' Cup final against Milan by the same score that Sunderland had inflicted. Before that European final Don Revie was reported to have held talks with Everton about taking over at Goodison Park despite his Leeds contract still having six years to run.

By the time QPR came to Roker Park Sunderland's players were understandably jiggered! The celebrations of the night before, the Monday night game at Cardiff, the coach travel and the emotional roller coaster of the cup final all took their toll against a quality side who wanted to show their promotion was no fluke. Before kick-off the Hoops were already nine points clear of third-placed Aston Villa who had completed their season. In front of a crowd of over 43,000 Sunderland's cup final XI took the game to the visitors for whom future England goalkeeper Phil Parkes was in top form.

The crowd had been outraged by QPR's Stan Bowles deliberately knocking the FA Cup off its perch by the side of the pitch early on and the refereeing performance of Mr Peter Reeves of Leicester had them infuriated. Eventually two thirds of the way into the match tiredness told and Rangers romped home with three goals in twelve minutes as the night deteriorated with at one point an irate supporter chasing the referee in the centre-circle having grabbed a corner flag to use as a weapon. Calm was quickly restored although referee Reeves remained persona non-grata on Wearside.

However, nothing could take away from the unforgettable scenes of the night before when finally after that lengthy wait for the cup heroes to return they had been afforded the most spectacularly enormous and heartfelt welcome. Having been away from home for ten days the players made the long coach journey home from Cardiff. Arriving in Carrville in Durham they transferred to an open-topped bus for the 13-mile journey to Roker Park.

It seemed as if everyone in the region had turned out to see the team and the cup. Even cows in the fields had red and white scarves on. People crowded into every available space to get the best vantage point. Amazingly and thankfully there were no known serious accidents as people climbed up onto roofs, stood on top of bus shelters and on branches of trees. By the time the team reached the town centre, upper storeys of shops where normally no-one would be were packed as any available space from which to witness Stokoe's Stars was claimed. The bus came along Fawcett Street, across Wearmouth Bridge and made its way to the final destination of Roker Park. Roker Park had been packed to the rafters long before the team got there. A carnival atmosphere prevailed. Having waited since 1937 for the cup to be won again no-one was worried about waiting an extra hour or two to see the trophy.

At one time it was normal for a team's demise, especially in the cup to be marked by the production of a Funeral card. These had been seen in Manchester as far back as 1912 after a Christmas week derby in which United beat City. Such cards remained in common use until the 1950s and were in evidence for example during Sunderland's cup-winning season of 1936-37.

After slaying Leeds someone had had the idea of parading a coffin bearing the words 'Leeds Died 1973' around Roker Park. In modern times of course this would be seen as very bad taste but at the time it was just intended as a light-hearted joke as opposed to anything sinister, one of the supporters carrying the coffin being dressed as a vicar.

In fact Sunderland supporters showed their style in sending almost 100 letters to Leeds United praising the Elland Road outfit's sportsmanship in accepting defeat graciously. Don Warters of the Yorkshire Evening Post reported a Leeds United spokesperson commenting, "We were surprised that so many people from Sunderland should take the time and the trouble to write to us saying how impressed they were with the way the club and our supporters had taken defeat. It was nice of them to do it and the letters were very much appreciated." Obviously disappointed, plenty of Leeds fans had welcomed the runners-up home on the day after the final.

WELL DONE SUNDERLAND

NCN 77L

73@FIFTY

Because of the game at Cardiff it took Sunderland a lot longer to return home but after the lengthy bus ride from Carrville when the team did eventually emerge from the Players' tunnel Roker Park erupted. When people talk about the Roker Roar they don't mean one particular roar, they mean the constant bedlam that would be produced as tens of thousands of Wearside voices would come together to roar the Lads on, that volume of noise often swirling on the winds blown in off the nearby North Sea. On this occasion it was one enormous roar as the players appeared. For as long as anyone but the oldest fans could remember that roar had been there to urge the players on to success. Not even the Bank of England Team of Len Shackleton, Billy Bingham, Ray Daniel and co had been able to achieve it but now this team; this team who had been near the bottom of the second division just before Christmas, had delivered the world's oldest and most glamorous trophy. And this to a town where the people had endured too many of the hard times both on the football pitch and in life, but now the whole world's eyes were on Sunderland.

In times to come the club would move to a new home called The Stadium of Light, but in 1973 the spotlight of the planet was on Sunderland. It was thanks to Bob Stokoe and his players. The supporters who welcomed the team home have never forgotten it and nor should they. The sons, daughters and grandchildren of those who experienced those wonderful and incredible few months have been brought up on tales of the Team of '73 and this footballing folklore will be passed on for many decades to come.

DENNIS TUEART

Wembley winner.

"There was no comparison between the homecoming I enjoyed at Sunderland and anything else I did in my career. It was a one-off. We had played at Cardiff on the Monday night and as we travelled home on the Tuesday we were told that we would get a good reception. The police had information about our route and timings. We freshened up at Scotch Corner and as we travelled up the motorway people were on bridges waiting for us. They must have waited there for ages and it would take us two seconds to go past and all we could do was give them a quick wave. We had a police escort and after we got onto the double-decker at Carrville it was just phenomenal. I can remember there were cows and horses with red and white colours tied to them. We were on the upper deck so we could see beyond the thousands of people lining the pavements. It was incredible."

RON GUTHRIE

Wembley winner.

"It was funny because my daughter's birthday was the day before the cup final. We got on a double decker at the A1 at Durham and I remember she had a face as long as a fiddle wondering what she was doing there? There were upwards of three-quarters of a million people to welcome us from Durham to Sunderland - and that's just people! I always remember there was even a horse in a field with a red and white strip on! I know for a fact there are SAFC supporters all over the shop, including all over Northumberland."

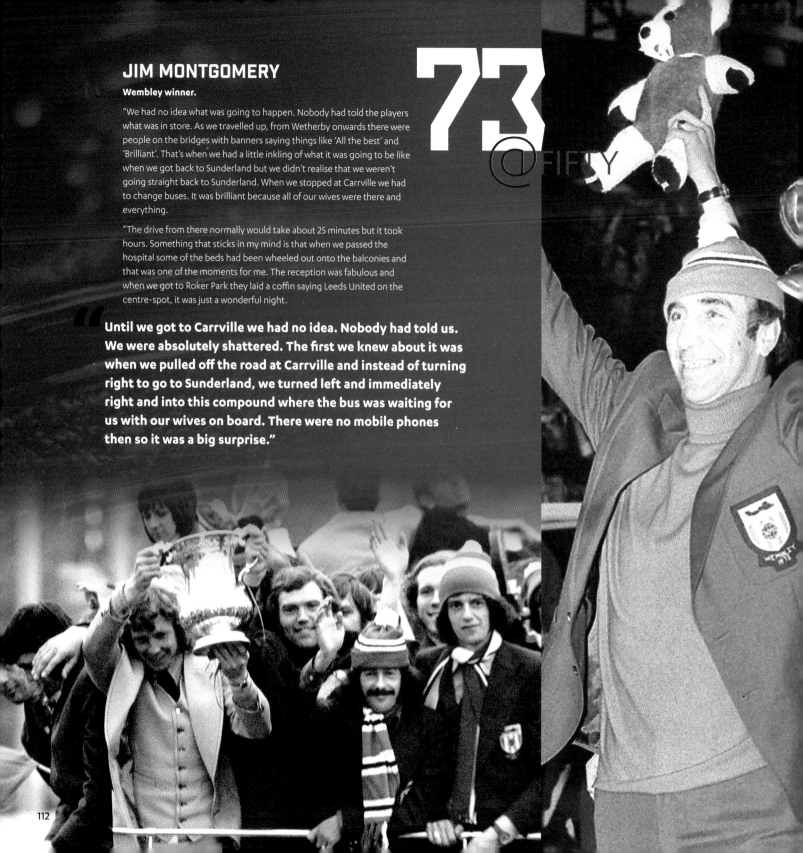

JIM MONTGOMERY

Wembley winner.

"We had no idea what was going to happen. Nobody had told the players what was in store. As we travelled up, from Wetherby onwards there were people on the bridges with banners saying things like 'All the best' and 'Brilliant'. That's when we had a little inkling of what it was going to be like when we got back to Sunderland but we didn't realise that we weren't going straight back to Sunderland. When we stopped at Carrville we had to change buses. It was brilliant because all of our wives were there and everything.

"The drive from there normally would take about 25 minutes but it took hours. Something that sticks in my mind is that when we passed the hospital some of the beds had been wheeled out onto the balconies and that was one of the moments for me. The reception was fabulous and when we got to Roker Park they laid a coffin saying Leeds United on the centre-spot, it was just a wonderful night.

"Until we got to Carrville we had no idea. Nobody had told us. We were absolutely shattered. The first we knew about it was when we pulled off the road at Carrville and instead of turning right to go to Sunderland, we turned left and immediately right and into this compound where the bus was waiting for us with our wives on board. There were no mobile phones then so it was a big surprise."

73@FIFTY

DICK MALONE

Wembley winner.

"I remember how dangerous it was with the crowds hanging from buildings in the town. I kept thinking people are going to fall. They were hanging out of windows and off roofs. I'm sure some of them must have had a few drinks and I was worried someone was going to get badly hurt.

The size of the crowds I couldn't believe and that was all the way from Carrville to Sunderland. The enormity of the crowds was unbelievable. If I'd been told there'll be massive crowds I could have believed it would be the case in the town centre and at Roker Park, but it was unbelievable all the way from Carrville.

"If you had caught everything on the journey from Carrville on film it would be worth 100 viewings. The amount of people there was incredible. As we went through the town centre there were people hanging from the rooftops! It was something that you would only dream of really and Jimmy is right, we had no idea we were about to take an open-topped bus ride from Carrville until we got there on our way back from the Monday night match at Cardiff."

MICK HORSWILL

Wembley winner.

"It was so emotional. When we came back we'd had a rough time in Cardiff the night before when they had a party for us after the game. Before we got to Carrville we stopped at Scotch Corner to go into the hotel to get washed and have a bit of a brush up and sober up because we thought, 'We can't let people see us in this state.' Some people changed their clothes and then we got to Carrville, got on the open-topped bus and from then on it was just amazing. I saw some of my mates on a wall and the whole journey was fantastic. It was one of the best parts of winning the cup.

"**Once we got to Roker Park when we walked onto the pitch there was a coffin in the centre-circle with 'Leeds United RIP' on it. The place was packed and it had taken us hours to get there. It was dangerous the way some people hung from roofs to see us but that's what it meant to people - and it meant just as much to us, and a lot of us were local lads.**

"We didn't realise what we'd done in terms of how much money came into Sunderland from around the world and we were told how much productivity had gone up in the shipyards and mines. It was massive but we were just young footballers and we didn't realise we'd caused all that. I just wish we could do it now. We were just ordinary people but people still ask me for autographs who are maybe only 20, but their dads make them watch DvDs of the cup final."

73

FIFTY

THE
STOKOE
STATUE

The wording on the front of the statue's plinth simply reads:

Bob Stokoe
1930-2004

Sunderland AFC Manager

The Man
The "Messiah"
The Moment…

1973 FA Cup winners
Sunderland AFC v Leeds United
5th May 1973

73 @ FIFTY

Along with the fans statue which pays tribute to the club's vast and loyal support, the only statue of an individual at the Stadium of Light is of Bob Stokoe. Sculpted by Sean Hedges-Quinn the statue captures a moment in time as the Messiah runs to Jim Montgomery in celebration at the end of the 1973 FA Cup final.

The statue was put in place on 18th July 2006, a couple of years after Stokoe passed away in 2004. It was unveiled by Bob's only child Karen, who kindly contributed the Foreword to this book and even more kindly provided the club with her father's tracksuit, mac and trilby from the cup final for permanent display in the entrance hall of the stadium.

As his daughter unveiled the statue, she was accompanied by Stokoe's skipper Bobby Kerr as well as Jim Montgomery, Dick Malone and Ritchie Pitt who, along with physio Johnny Watters all came to pay tribute to the man who inspired the greatest cup story of them all.

An appeal to raise £73,000 to pay for the statue attracted donations large and small from a wide range of organisations and individuals, all of whom wanted to recognise Stokoe's enormous contribution to north east football. Some of the proceeds came from a beer called 'Bob Stokoe's Best' produced by the Double Maxim Beer Company.

There was even a donation from the Former Players' Association of Newcastle United, Bob of course having also won the FA Cup as a player with the Magpies in 1955.

On the day the statue was unveiled Karen commented, "I'm very pleased with the statue and have been so impressed with the efforts of the committee and people of Sunderland in their fund raising efforts. It is nice to know my father is still held in such high regard."

No one could be a better judge of the statue than the man Stokoe was sprinting towards at the instant captured in the artwork, Jim Montgomery. He noted...

" It's terrific. Bob was running towards me at that moment and the statue really captures the excitement and emotion."

Summing up the way the statue provides a lasting legacy to the man who found the magic that inspired the cup triumph Ritchie Pitt remarked...

"It is a fitting tribute and very realistic. I wish Bob could have been alive to see it but the important thing is that supporters now and in the future will be able to see the statue whenever they are at the Stadium of Light and it will always mean a great deal to them."

73 @FIFTY

THE CHARITY SHIELD

Sunderland chose not to take part in the Charity Shield. League champions Liverpool also declined their invitation in the last year before the season curtain-raiser was moved to Wembley. Instead second division champions Burnley took on Manchester City at Maine Road, City having finished 11th in Division One. The Clarets took the trophy having won 1-0 with a goal from future Sunderland defender Colin Waldron.

For their part FA Cup holders Sunderland staged a pre-season fixture with League Cup holders Spurs, both clubs parading their trophies before a game with Tottenham won 1-0 with a goal from Jimmy Neighbour.

WHATEVER HAPPENED TO
THE LIKELY
LADS

Written by a writing duo that
included Ian La Frenais who
was born in the north east in
1937, the year that Raich Carter
and co first won the FA Cup for
Sunderland, 'The Likely Lads'
was a top British sitcom that ran
in the mid-sixties and was then
revived in 1973, first airing four
days before Sunderland's cup run
commenced at Notts County.
One of its two stars was
Sunderland-born actor
James Bolam.

JIM MONTGOMERY WITH PETER RODRIGUES AT SOUTHAMPTON

73

@FIFTY

As the cup final took place Bolam was on stage in a performance of an award winning play, 'Butley' by Simon Gray but proclaimed himself, "Over the moon" that Sunderland were at Wembley and said, "Bob Stokoe has done a marvellous job since he took over at Roker Park". As for Sunderland's 'Likely Lads' whatever happened to the cup winners?

JIM MONTGOMERY

Magnificent Monty went on to establish a club record 627 appearances, a massive 169 more games than anyone else has ever played for the club. Astonishingly the last of these matches took place when Jim was still only 33, a young age for a keeper.

A loan at Southampton was followed by a spell with Birmingham City where he played for England's 1966 FIFA World Cup winning manager Sir Alf Ramsey and a stint with Nottingham Forest under his old Sunderland colleague Brian Clough where he won a European Cup winners' medal as an unused sub in 1980.

Monty had a second period at Sunderland without adding to his total of first-team games. He managed Meadowfield Sports Centre in Durham and coached goalkeepers at numerous clubs including Sunderland where he returned once again to run the youth team. Jim became chairman of the SAFC Former Players' Association and club ambassador. The main banqueting suite at the Stadium of Light was named the Montgomery Suite in his honour and he was awarded the British Empire Medal in 2016 and the Freedom of the City of Sunderland in 2016. In the 2022-23 season his grandson James Montgomery kept goal for Gateshead in the first round of the FA Cup.

THE TV LIKELY LADS:
RODNEY BEWES AND JAMES BOLAM

MONTY, BACK ROW THIRD FROM RIGHT, AT BIRMINGHAM CITY
THREE TO JIM'S RIGHT IS FUTURE SAFC MANAGER RICKY SBRAGIA

DICK MALONE

After Sunderland, Dick went on to play for Hartlepool, Blackpool (under Bob Stokoe), Queen of the South (where he won promotion under ex-Sunderland midfielder George Herd) and finally North Shields. He also had a spell managing Horden CW before going into business, including working in haulage.

Malone gave great service as a committee member of the Former Players' Association and worked extensively in corporate hospitality back at SAFC. Like the rest of the outfield players from the cup final (Montgomery having already received the award), Dick received the Freedom of the City of Sunderland in 2022.

RON GUTHRIE

After Sunderland, Ron played for Gateshead, Lusitano in South Africa as player/manager, Blyth Spartans and North Shields. His FA Cup exploits continued when he helped Blyth reach the fifth round five years after winning the trophy with Sunderland.

Following his retirement from the game Guthrie became a milkman on Tyneside before re-uniting with his former full-back partner Dick Malone with a delivery firm. Ron went on to find employment as a delivery driver for Fenwicks Department store in Newcastle.

MICKY HORSWILL

Micky went on to play for Manchester City, Plymouth Argyle, Hull City, Happy Valley in Hong Kong, Barrow (under the management of Vic Halom) and Carlisle United where he was re-united with Bob Stokoe.

Micky later became a publican and ran a sports and social club attached to the Nissan car plant. He managed Thorney Close Variety Club, worked as a sales rep for a worktop supplier in Shildon and became transport manager for a flooring and kitchen worktop company. Horswill also became a popular radio personality alongside club legends from Newcastle United and Middlesbrough. Often involved in charity work and a keen golfer, Mick became chairman of the Sunderland Former Players' Association and worked back at the club in corporate hospitality.

In addition to books published as part of his role as one of 'The Three Legends' radio show in 2015 Mick also produced a book entitled, "Micky's Top 50 Sunderland AFC Players of His Generation."

73 @FIFTY

73

WHATEVER HAPPENED TO THE LIKELY LADS

DAVE WATSON

Watson went on to total 65 caps for England, the first 14 having been won with Sunderland. After leaving Wearside he starred for Manchester City and continued his career with Werder Bremen, Southampton, Stoke City, Vancouver Whitecaps, Derby County, Fort Lauderdale, Notts County and Kettering Town.

After retiring, Dave ran a successful company arranging events and speaking engagements for former footballers. In 2021 Dave won a landmark ruling to have injuries suffered during his playing days to be classed as industrial accidents. Dave's story was told in wife Penny's book 'My Dear Watson' published in 1981.

127

RITCHIE PITT

The second youngest member of the team, Ritchie was the first to finish his football career. In his case this was through injury early in the season after the FA Cup triumph. He had a joint testimonial with fellow injury victim Bobby Park at Sunderland. Pitt recovered to carve out another successful career, this time in education. Along with Jim Montgomery and Micky Horswill, Ritchie became one of a trio of cup winners to later serve as chairman of the Former Players' Association.

BOBBY KERR

Captain Kerr went on to play for Blackpool, Hartlepool United and Whitby Town, working with Bob Stokoe once again whilst with the Tangerines.

Following retirement he sold insurance before becoming a publican, running the Park Inn near Park Lane bus station in Sunderland, the Hastings Hill and the Copt Hill at Houghton-le-Spring. Ever popular, Kerr continued his captain's duties in 2022 when speaking on behalf of his teammates in accepting the Freedom of the City of Sunderland award. Bobby had been the last of the cup-winning team to play a game for Sunderland, his valedictory appearance coming in August 1978 - barely five years after that most glorious of days in 1973. Bobby's book, 'The Little General' was published in 2013.

VIC HALOM

Oldham Athletic, Arcadia Shepherds (South Africa), Rotherham United (where he was player/coach under Ian Porterfield) and Northwich Victoria were Halom's post-Sunderland clubs as a player. He moved to Norway to become coach of Frederikstad before managing Barrow and Rochdale. After a short spell working for his home town club Burton Albion Halom worked for Ferrodo before returning to football as Commercial Manager and director of North Shields.

There followed a 23-year spell working for New Earth Water Services, ten of those years being spent in Mexico with a shorter period based in Aden. In more recent years Vic has spent much of his time living in Bulgaria, looking to scout and recruit players from there and surrounding countries. In 1992 Vic even found the time to stand for Parliament in Sunderland North for the Liberal Democrats, finishing third.

73

VIC, BACK ROW THIRD FROM RIGHT, IN AN OLDHAM ATHLETIC TEAM GROUP

RITCHIE PITT, BOBBY KERR AND VIC HALOM

129

BILLY HUGHES

Billy played for Derby County, Leicester City, Carlisle United (under
Bob Stokoe, on loan), San Jose and Corby Town after leaving Wearside.
He was also capped by Scotland whilst still with the red and whites.

**While at Sunderland he had a shoe-shop called Billy's Shughes.
After retiring Billy became a licensee in Derby, club house manager
at Stressholme Golf Club in Darlington and later ran Keddleston Park
Golf Club in Derby. Billy passed away in December 2019.**

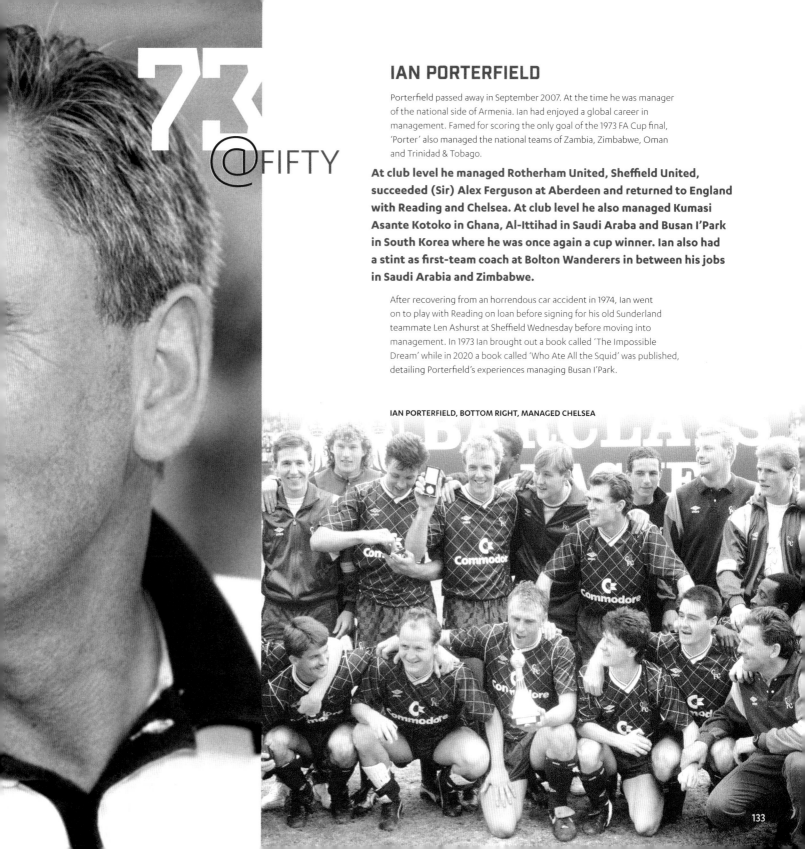

73@FIFTY

IAN PORTERFIELD

Porterfield passed away in September 2007. At the time he was manager of the national side of Armenia. Ian had enjoyed a global career in management. Famed for scoring the only goal of the 1973 FA Cup final, 'Porter' also managed the national teams of Zambia, Zimbabwe, Oman and Trinidad & Tobago.

At club level he managed Rotherham United, Sheffield United, succeeded (Sir) Alex Ferguson at Aberdeen and returned to England with Reading and Chelsea. At club level he also managed Kumasi Asante Kotoko in Ghana, Al-Ittihad in Saudi Araba and Busan I'Park in South Korea where he was once again a cup winner. Ian also had a stint as first-team coach at Bolton Wanderers in between his jobs in Saudi Arabia and Zimbabwe.

After recovering from an horrendous car accident in 1974, Ian went on to play with Reading on loan before signing for his old Sunderland teammate Len Ashurst at Sheffield Wednesday before moving into management. In 1973 Ian brought out a book called 'The Impossible Dream' while in 2020 a book called 'Who Ate All the Squid' was published, detailing Porterfield's experiences managing Busan I'Park.

IAN PORTERFIELD, BOTTOM RIGHT, MANAGED CHELSEA

133

DENNIS TUEART

Leaving Sunderland for Manchester City, Dennis added a League Cup winner's medal to his FA Cup one. As a teammate of Dave Watson Dennis scored the most famous goal from any League Cup final with a spectacular bicycle-kick that helped defeat his hometown team Newcastle United in 1976.

Capped six times by England, Dennis was later signed by New York Cosmos to replace no less a figure than Pelé. Tueart also turned out for Stoke City, Burnley and briefly for Derry City (for his old Sunderland youth team colleague Eamonn McLaughlin), as well as having a second spell in the blue half of Manchester where he also became a director.

Successful in business, Dennis moved from being a sales director for a sports promotions company to creating his own Premier Events Company Ltd. Dennis published his autobiography, 'My Football Journey' in 2011 with all royalties going to the Christie cancer centre in Manchester.

73

@FIFTY

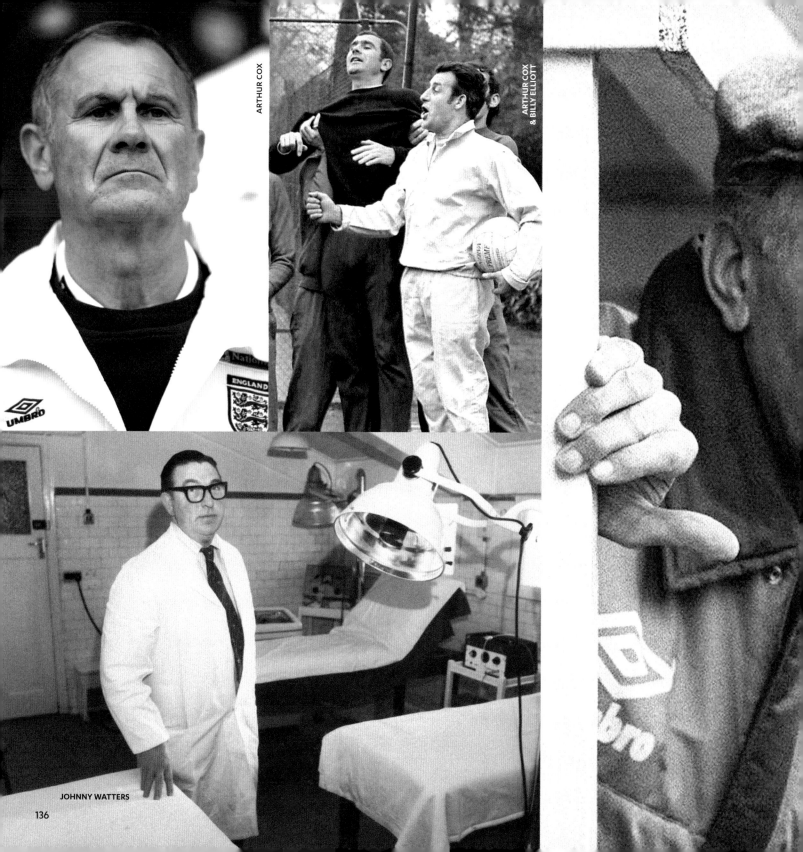

ARTHUR COX

ARTHUR COX & BILLY ELLIOTT

JOHNNY WATTERS

DAVID YOUNG

David went on to play for Charlton Athletic, Southend United and Dartford before working in sports centre management in Orpington, Bexleyheath and Gillingham.

BOB STOKOE

After guiding Sunderland to the Division Two title in 1976 Stokoe went on to manage Bury, Blackpool, Rochdale, Carlisle. These were all clubs he had managed before which is a testament to how highly he was thought of.

He also returned to Sunderland for a second spell when he took over from Lawrie McMenemy as he tried to stave off the club's relegation. Bob's biography, 'Northern and Proud' was published in 2009 five years after he passed away.

ARTHUR COX

First-team coach. Arthur went on to manage Chesterfield, Newcastle United and Derby County. Having brought Kevin Keegan to Tyneside Arthur also later worked with Keegan at Fulham and with England before becoming assistant manager at Manchester City and first team coach back at Newcastle when reunited with Keegan.

BILLY ELLIOTT

Having helped Sunderland to win the FA Cup, former England international Elliott went on to manage FC Brann to the cup in Norway in 1976. He returned to Sunderland and had a half season spell as caretaker manager in 1978-79 before spending four years in charge of Darlington. Billy passed away in 2008.

JOHNNY WATTERS

The physiotherapist with the magic sponge, former Celtic player Watters was always a great character at Sunderland where he gave almost three decades worth of service from 1955 until his retirement in 1983. Johnny passed away in 2012.

DAVID YOUNG

BILLY ELLIOTT, BOB STOKOE, ARTHUR COX & JOHNNY WATTERS

73 @FIFTY

FA CUP WINNERS
FREEDOM
OF THE CITY

The thirteenth of January 2022 saw the Team of 73 honoured with the Freedom of the City of Sunderland. Bob Stokoe and the club itself were recognised by the Borough of Sunderland on 21 January 1974 while on 12 May 2016 I was delighted to be invited by Jim Montgomery to be one of his guests when Jim received the Freedom of the City along with John Hays of Hays Travel, a former vice-chairman of SAFC when Niall Quinn was chairman. In December 2019 I put forward the idea that the rest of the FA Cup winning team of 1973 should also be recognised for their achievement with the award of the Freedom of the City.

I was pushing at an open door. As soon as I put forward the proposal with the assistance of Sunderland's then head of media Louise Wanless, the council agreed in principle immediately. I was asked to liaise with the players but to ask them to keep the news confidential until the council were ready to formally announce the award. Initially we had to wait until the appropriate committees of the council met to formally approve the idea but then covid struck. For over a year we hoped to arrange a date for the ceremony but every time it looked like we might be able to, one covid-related reason or another caused a postponement.

In the meantime local councillor Michael Dixon, a long-standing Sunderland supporter, made an additional proposal that a further joint award was made to those players who had played in the earlier rounds. Consequently a joint award was made to five of those players who accepted the honour.

When the ceremony finally took place, the date of 13 January 2022 was chosen because it was the 49th anniversary of the first match of the cup run at Notts County. By then it might be wondered why we didn't wait until the 50th anniversary? The straight-forward answer to that is that having already lost Ian Porterfield and Billy Hughes from the cup-winning team more than one of the others was not in the best of health with dementia in particular a danger to their well-being.

Given the contemporary debates about the effect of heading on the dementia rates of former footballers you may have your own thoughts on this. As was already publicly known at the time Dave Watson was already suffering, his wife Penny becoming a leading light in the 'Head for Change' campaign which looks to explore the links between football and dementia.

Arguably significantly, Watson was a centre-half and centre-forward throughout his career, positions of course where you do more heading than any other positions. Watson was Sunderland's centre-half at Wembley. Centre-forward Vic Halom remembers, "When I was a young player at Charlton in training I'd have to head a ball hung from a rope for an hour at a time." Another centre-forward in the cup squad - John Lathan who played in the third and fourth rounds before Halom was signed - has long been in the position whereby when I have a video call with him at his home in Manhattan, New York, John's wife Lauren often has to prompt him regarding things he can't recall - even if we have discussed it in the previous hour.

Lathan and his wife travelled from New York for the ceremony which was attended by all surviving members of the cup-winning team bar Micky Horswill who unfortunately had to drop out at the last moment through illness. Jim Montgomery accepted Mick's award. Of the two members of the team sadly no longer with us at the time of the ceremony Billy Hughes was represented by his widow Linda while goalscorer Ian Porterfield's award was collected by his grandson Callum Porterfield.

Of the players to receive the joint award for playing in rounds before the final John Lathan, Jackie Ashurst and Mick McGiven attended, McGiven accepting the award on their behalf. Brian Chambers (who was an unused sub in the semi-final) was also due to attend but, like Horswill, had to drop out shortly before the ceremony for health reasons. The last of the five to receive this award was John Tones. Unable to attend due to living in Melbourne Australia he was represented by family and friends.

Defenders Keith Coleman and Joe Bolton also played in the FA Cup run but politely declined the joint award. Cult hero Bolton has always been a very private person while Cyprus-based Coleman still feels hard done to by Bob Stokoe and courteously declined to be listed as one of the joint recipients.

While Keith and Joe didn't want to be involved all those who attended were delighted to be recognised. "It's a great honour" said Ritchie Pitt. "As a lad from Plains Farm Estate to be recognised by your home town is fantastic. I'm so proud to have the award."

73

@FIFTY

MAYOR COUNCILLOR HENRY TRUEMAN HANDS THE JOINT AWARD TO (LEFT TO RIGHT) JOHN LATHAN, MICK McGIVEN, JACKIE ASHURST AND JOHN TONES' REPRESENTATIVE PETER GIBSON

THE TEAM OF 73 ON THE NIGHT OF THE FREEDOM OF THE CITY AWARDS.
LEFT TO RIGHT: DENNIS TUEART, VIC HALOM, RON GUTHRIE, DAVE WATSON,
BOBBY KERR (FRONT), DICK MALONE, JIM MONTGOMERY, RITCHIE PITT (RED JACKET),
JOHN LATHAN (FRONT), DAVID YOUNG, JACKIE ASHURST, MICK McGIVEN

DAVID YOUNG

RON GUTHRIE

VIC HALOM

DICK MALONE

CALLUM PORTERFIELD ON
BEHALF OF HIS GRANDFATHER

DENNIS TUEART

DAVE WATSON

Jackie Ashurst commented, "It was great, fantastic to see all the lads again. A lot of them were in the juniors when I came to the club and I hadn't seen many of them for a lot of years. We all got on well together so it was really good to meet up again as a group. Getting some recognition was one of the main things about it. I was basically too young to be playing on a regular basis but I got involved in the earlier rounds playing against Notts County and Reading."

Captain Bobby Kerr said, "It's been a long time coming but to be honest it's nice to be honoured by the town I've lived in since I was 15. It's a real honour for me."

Before the awards were handed out several councillors spoke. These included Councillor Dixon who reflected, "It was a moving experience for me to speak at the Awards Ceremony, especially as I had played a part in ensuring the contributions of the early round players were recognised. Many travelled far and wide to attend it meant that much to them." Once the awards had been received it was left to captain Bobby Kerr and myself, as the club historian and person behind the main proposal to offer speeches of thanks.

Sunderland City Council leader Graeme Miller put the seal on the event by saying of the players, "The esteem in which these gentlemen are held is unparalleled in this devoted, football loving city. So although 49 years have passed since that glorious trophy was lifted I understand completely how the pride, passion and joyous memory of that magnificent day and incredible achievement have not dimmed one bit - either for the supporters and indeed the vast majority of Sunderland people, or the squad members themselves.

BILLY HUGHES' WIDOW LINDA PROUDLY RECEIVED BILLY'S AWARD

RITCHIE PITT

BOBBY KERR

TEAM CAPTAIN BOBBY KERR WHO GAVE A HEARTFELT THANK YOU SPEECH ON BEHALF OF THE PLAYERS

AUTHOR OF THIS BOOK AND CLUB HISTORIAN ROB MASON SPOKE ABOUT THE REASONS FOR THE AWARDS

EE AYE ADDIO
WE WON THE CUP!